More Twist-and-Turn Bargello Quilts

STRIP PIECE 10 NEW PROJECTS   EILEEN WRIGHT

Martingale
Create with Confidence

Dedication

To all of the quilters who found a way to contact me with
their requests. If not for you, this book wouldn't exist.

More Twist-and-Turn Bargello Quilts:
Strip Piece 10 New Projects
© 2013 by Eileen Wright

Martingale®
19021 120th Ave. NE, Ste. 102
Bothell, WA 98011-9511 USA
ShopMartingale.com

Printed in China
18 17 16 15 14 13   8 7 6 5 4 3 2

Library of Congress Cataloging-in-Publication Data
is available upon request.

ISBN: 978-1-60468-259-5

MISSION STATEMENT

Dedicated to providing quality products
and service to inspire creativity.

CREDITS

President and CEO: Tom Wierzbicki
Editor in Chief: Mary V. Green
Design Director: Paula Schlosser
Managing Editor: Karen Costello Soltys
Acquisitions Editor: Karen M. Burns
Technical Editor: Nancy Mahoney
Copy Editor: Marcy Heffernan
Production Manager: Regina Girard
Cover and Interior Designer: Adrienne Smitke
Photographer: Brent Kane
Illustrators: Kathryn Conway and Lisa Lauch

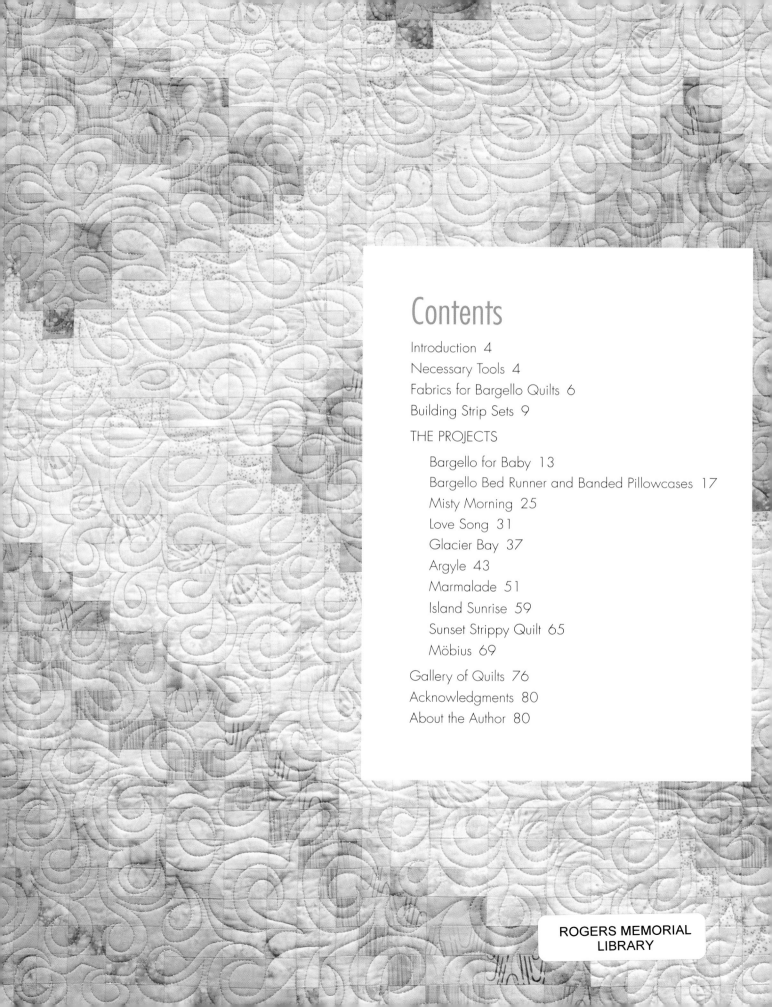

Contents

Introduction

All of the bargello quilts in this book are made using regular strip-piecing techniques and a range of fabrics that produce a gradation of color in light to dark order. I prefer a color-wash effect, an even gradation of value from one fabric to the next, in my fabric runs wherever possible, and I always gravitate toward batiks because of the vibrant colors.

Assigning numbers to the fabrics in light to dark order, and then following a numbered chart (sort of like a paint-by-number map) allows the fabrics to be rearranged out of numerical sequence so that the design changes shape and direction, wiggling and twisting to form an exciting new design or secondary image. Varying widths of slices cut from the strip sets help to produce rounder curves as well as sharper points within the overall quilt design.

In this book I share the methods that work best for me. I encourage you to use what you like and create your own best methods along the way. There is always more than one right way to do things in quilting.

Necessary Tools

Good work requires good equipment. At a minimum, you'll need a sewing machine in good working order with a ¼" patchwork foot. If you're master of your machine, the process of creating a quilt or any stitched item will be that much easier.

Cutting Tools

You'll require a solid surface to use as a cutting table, whether it's the dining table, a section of kitchen counter, or a specially made cutting table that's tall enough to reduce back strain caused by constantly bending to cut fabrics. The kitchen counter is higher than dining tables, so it makes a suitable place to cut fabric if you can snatch a corner of it for quilting purposes. Obviously a dedicated cutting space is ideal, but my experience has shown that sewists and quilters are creative. We'll find a space that works.

The bed-sized quilts in this book require a cutting mat that is at least 24" x 36". You'll also need a 24"-long ruler and a rotary cutter with a sharp blade. Extra mats and rulers are nice to have if you're a prolific quilter.

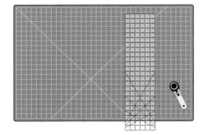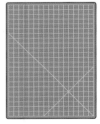

Pressing Equipment

Because pressing is so important to the finished result of any project, you'll also need a good solid ironing board without a lot of padding. If you have a handy carpenter-type person in your life, you might wish to have him or her make a larger pressing surface to fit on top of your regular ironing board. You'll need a piece of plywood cut to the size of rectangle you want, making it slightly larger than your ironing board. On the underneath side of the plywood, use 1" x 1" wood strips along the edges of the plywood to frame the rectangle and secure it to your ironing board. Cover the top of the plywood with one or two layers of cotton batting and a single layer of muslin wrapped to the back edge and stapled firmly in place. This type of firm surface, combined with a good-quality steam iron, makes easy work of the many seam allowances in a bargello quilt.

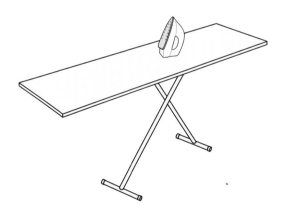

Needles and Threads

Always match your sewing-machine thread to your fabric content. A 50-weight 100% cotton thread in a neutral shade (such as gray) works best for strip piecing 100% cotton fabrics. I only change my thread color if I'm sewing white or black fabrics. Similarly you need a needle size that works with the fabric and thread weight that you're using. A sharp 80/12 does the job nicely.

Batting

When it comes to quilt batting, most quilters eventually find a favorite. I've tried a few varieties, including wool and the newer bamboo blends, but my personal favorite is a bleached 80/20 cotton/polyester blend manufactured by Hobbs Quilt Batting. It's lightweight, has a lovely loft, and drapes nicely. To me, it looks the best when quilted, and it's cozy and comfortable to sleep under. If you prefer a 100% polyester batting, be sure to choose one that has been heat bonded rather than chemically bonded for safety, and is guaranteed not to beard through your cotton fabrics.

Miscellaneous Supplies

You'll also need basic sewing accessories: scissors, thread snips, straight pins, pencils, chalk markers, and a seam ripper, at a minimum. I also find a stiletto or awl handy to use while joining the rows, but the point of a seam ripper can be used in a pinch. The gadget lovers among you will no doubt add to this list of basics.

In addition, I find a Ruby Beholder® and a green value finder are handy tools for sorting fabrics into light-to-dark sequences. Quilt shops often have these on hand for your use while shopping.

Choosing the fabrics for any new project is the most exciting part for me—except for seeing the quilt actually finished. But we have to make a start before we can get to the end. Don't be intimidated when you read that you need 20 fabrics for some of these quilts (or 30 fabrics for "Marmalade" on page 51). There are so many ways to reach the desired goal.

First you need to decide what color or theme you want to incorporate into your vision of the chosen design. You can decide on either one or two colors and pull every possible fabric from your own stash, or go to your favorite quilt shop and see what inspires you from the fabric selection currently available. Even if you choose the second option, I encourage you to use as many fabrics as possible from your stash. It can help to keep the guilt at bay if your stash is getting out of hand.

In addition, do keep an open mind to fabrics that seem to fit but are just a bit unusual or out of your usual comfort zone. The inclusion of one or two fabrics that fit that description will probably be the fabrics that make your quilt sing. Always be on the lookout for a few of those fabrics that I like to call zingers. They really contribute to a great end result and will make your project sparkle. To me, a zinger fabric is one that is a bit wilder and may not be a perfect match, but it still blends in color and/or value with the overall fabric lineup.

When choosing fabrics for your quilt, trust your instincts and create your own vision of any of these designs. Let your creativity loose. There are no rules when it comes to the fabrics you use in your quilts. You only have to please yourself.

Organizing Fabrics by Value

Once you've accumulated a large selection of fabrics, sort them into a stack of lights to darks for a one-color quilt or into a light-to-dark stack for each color group in a two-color quilt.

Value is relative, so arranging fabrics in order from light to dark can sometimes be challenging. It can be difficult to determine the value of a print or batik that has various colors or values or is a high-contrast print (dark motifs on light background, for instance). A Ruby Beholder is helpful for assessing value. This dark-red plastic tool can be used to view the relative value in fabric. When you look at your fabrics through the plastic, the colors disappear, and you're left looking at shades of light and dark. However, this tool doesn't work with red-toned fabrics. Instead, try using a green value finder.

Sixteen green batiks, organized from lightest value to darkest.

Another way to determine the value of a fabric is to arrange your fabrics in sequence from light to dark, with about 1" of each fabric showing. Then photocopy the fabrics in black and white. The resulting image in shades of gray can help you easily see if you need to rearrange any fabrics to get the correct light-to-dark order. Sometimes standing back and squinting at the pile of fabrics will work for testing value too. Use whichever method works best for you.

If you're still really unsure, seek the assistance of a quilt-shop employee or a talented quilting friend. If you're purchasing all the fabrics for a project, one of the shop's staff members would probably enjoy helping you make your selections. Even if you take fabrics from your stash into a shop to use as a starting point, they won't mind helping add to your selection. Quilt-shop staff usually share our addiction to color and fabric, and understand that quilters collect fabric and need to use fabrics from their stash from time to time.

Once you've determined the correct order of your fabric lineup, take a digital picture or label the fabrics in some way, especially if you still have to wash them. You can even use a permanent marker to write the sequence number in the selvage if all else fails.

STRIVE FOR EVEN GRADATION

My feeling is that a fairly even gradation of value from one fabric to the next produces the most pleasing end result. I prefer a smooth blend of values rather than a striped look. But any time you use more than one color you're probably going to create a bit of striping. For the most part, trust your own instincts about color. It's your quilt, and it should please you— not necessarily the shop person or anyone else. (Unless the quilt is to be a gift, in which case you might have to think like the intended recipient.)

Preparing the Fabrics

To wash or not to wash fabrics is a subject of much debate and personal choice. I don't believe I can change the mind of anyone who doesn't prewash their fabrics. Personally, every fabric that comes into my home goes directly to the laundry closet to be soaked in cold water, spun, and dried in a hot dryer. I believe it's the dryer that does the shrinking.

If I have any concerns about color running, then I set the color with a product called Retayne, which is available at most quilt shops. Just follow the instructions on the bottle.

When your fabric comes out of the dryer, fold it in half lengthwise, matching the selvages and making sure there are no twists or wrinkles along the fold. Press the fabric while it's folded in half, being careful not to press over the fold line, only up to it. If you press the fold, you'll probably never be able to remove the crease. Once your fabric is folded on grain and well pressed, it's ready to be cut into the required strips for your project.

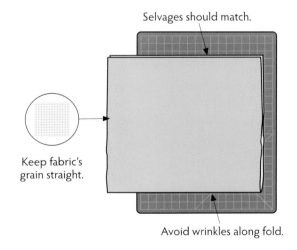

Selvages should match.

Keep fabric's grain straight.

Avoid wrinkles along fold.

Cutting Straight Strips

Cutting strips at an exact right angle to the folded edge of your fabric is essential for making accurate strip sets.

Place your pressed fabric on your cutting mat with the folded edge nearest to your body. Place the ruler on top of the fabric along the right edge, aligning a line on the ruler with the fabric fold. The raw, uneven edges should extend beyond the ruler's edge, as shown. Cut along the long edge of the ruler to trim off the end of the fabric, making a straight edge. This is known as a clean-up cut. (Reverse this procedure if you're left-handed.) Save the little bit of fabric removed by the clean-up cut; this nice snippet can be used to create the fabric map required for your project. See "Creating a Fabric Map" at right.

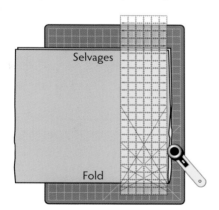

Now carefully turn the fabric over, placing the straightened edge to your left and the fold at the bottom. Cut the strips in the width specified in the project instructions; measure from the straight edge. For example, if you need 2"-wide strips, place the 2" line on the ruler on the straightened edge of the fabric and cut along the ruler's right edge.

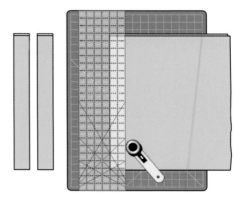

Creating a Fabric Map

You'll need a snippet of each bargello fabric, arranged in light-to-dark order, with assigned numbers. Tape or glue the snippets to a sheet of white paper in numerical sequence and write the corresponding number above each fabric. This is your fabric map, and it's critical to the successful completion of all of the designs in this book.

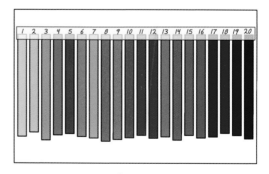

Fabric map

Building Strip Sets

Bargello quilts are made by cutting fabric strips to the required width, sewing the strips together in the predetermined sequence, and then cutting the strip sets into slices. A straight, accurate scant ¼" seam allowance is used for all the projects in this book. When the slices are sewn together, the beauty of the pattern emerges, but it all starts with building strip sets.

1. Set your sewing machine to a smaller-than-normal stitch length (such as 2.0 mm) to prevent the seams of the cut slices from opening as you work with them.
2. Cut the number of fabric strips in the required width from each designated fabric for the specific project you're making.
3. Lay out the fabric strips in stacks, one for each fabric, in the order in which they'll be sewn. Fabric 1 will be on the left and fabric 20 on the right as shown.

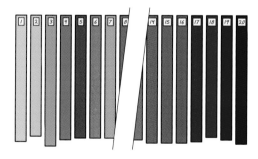

4. Lay a fabric 2 strip on top of a fabric 1 strip, right sides together and raw edges aligned. Sew the strips together along their long right-hand edge using a scant ¼"-wide seam allowance.

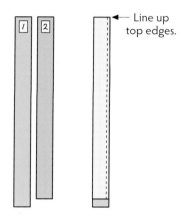

Line up top edges.

5. Continue in the same manner, sewing the strips into pairs, making sure the even-numbered strip is always on top.
6. Referring to your fabric map, sew the strip pairs together in the order in which they're numbered. Always flip the higher number over onto the lower number, right sides together, and sew down the right-hand edge. Referring to "Preventing Strip Sets from Bowing" on page 10, continue joining the strips until they're all sewn into one complete strip set.

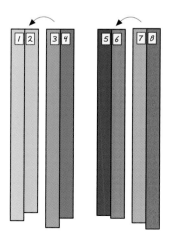

Sew strip pairs together.

7. Build the number of strip sets in the correct numerical sequence as indicated in the instructions for your project. Note that for some of the projects, you'll need more strip sets of some fabrics than others. In these cases, you'll be instructed to build extra strip sets using only a partial lineup of the fabrics.

Preventing Strip Sets From Bowing

Bowing is a common problem when creating strip sets. Reversing the sewing direction from one strip to the next will help prevent the strips from curving.

Sew the strips in pairs as instructed in "Building Strip Sets" and press the seam allowances in the direction indicated in the project instructions. In most of the projects the seam allowances are pressed toward the even-numbered fabrics. To maximize the number of slices, you'll want to keep the strips even on one end of the completed strip set. To do this and still prevent the strip sets from bowing, start by arranging the strip pairs in the correct sequence and line up the end you're keeping even. When sewing the strip pairs together, flip the pairs over and sew from the uneven end.

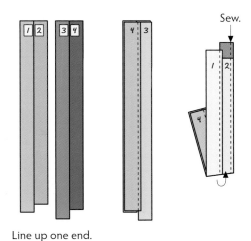

Line up one end.

After sewing the first set of strip pairs together, you'll be sewing from the uneven end until all strip pairs are sewn into a single strip set.

Pressing

Proper pressing is also critical to the success of strip piecing. I like to use steam for this process, as it helps sets the seam firmly in place. I also prefer a very hard ironing board, instead of one with a lot of padding.

1. Press each stack of strip pairs immediately after stitching, before sewing the strip pairs together. Lay the strip set on the ironing board with the seam allowances away from you. The fabric on top is the one the seam allowances will be pressed toward. For example, for strip pairs of fabrics 1 and 2, if you want the seam allowances pressed toward the lower number (1), make sure fabric 1 is on top. Similarly, if you want the seam allowances pressed toward the higher number, position the pair with the fabric 2 on top.

2. Position the strips along the length of your ironing board, with the line of stitching as straight as possible. Press the seam flat from the wrong side to set the stitches and remove any puckers.

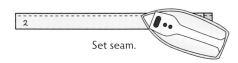

Set seam.

3. Flip the top piece over, right side up, and run your finger along the seam line ahead of the iron, taking care to keep your fingers out of the way of the iron and steam. Use the side of the iron to gently push the top strip over the seam allowance. Do not wiggle the iron back and forth. Instead, hold it in place for a couple of seconds to firmly press the seam. Work your way along the entire strip in this manner.

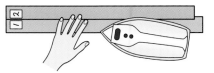

Push fabric away from seam with side of iron.

4. Make sure the unit is lying straight on the board, and once more press the strip pair along the seam line from the right side.

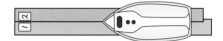

PRESSING DIRECTION

Pressing the seam allowances in the correct direction is critical in order to accurately match seam lines, and the direction has been carefully thought out ahead of time. Press the strips in the direction indicated in the instructions for the project you're making; this way the seam allowances will oppose each other and neatly butt against each other (or nest) when you're sewing the rows together. With a bit of practice, you'll be able to wiggle the seam intersections into a perfect match and stitch without using pins. Honest.

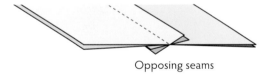

Opposing seams

Cutting Slices

1. Fold a strip set in half wrong side out along the center seam line. Lay it on your cutting mat as shown in step 2, making sure that all the seams are straight, smooth, and parallel. Nest the seam allowances of each row, and then pin the top raw edges together using about four straight pins across the 42" width.

2. Trim the selvages on the right, uneven end of the strip set by carefully aligning a horizontal line on the cutting ruler with one of the strip set's internal seam lines. Be sure to remove any pins that lie under or near your ruler before cutting.

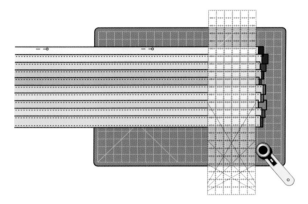

3. Place the straightened end on the left, align the desired measurement on your cutting ruler with the straightened end, and cut. Cut the number of slices required in the width indicated for each row of your project. If your ruler is shorter than the width of your folded strip set, slide your ruler the distance needed, keeping the edge of the ruler even with the cut edge, and continue cutting.

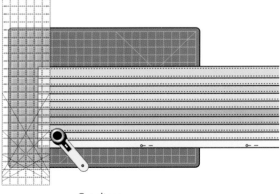

Cut slices.

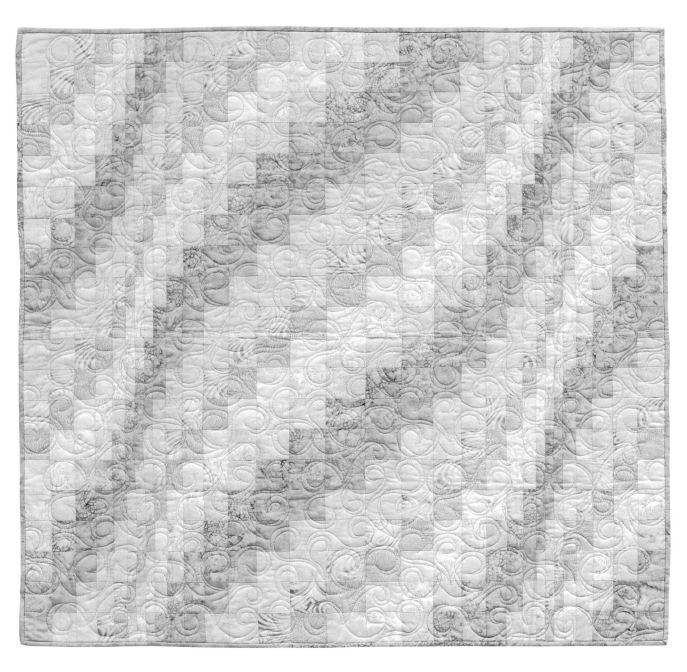

Pieced by author and quilted by Fran Henney of Parksville, British Columbia, Canada

FINISHED SIZE: 39½" x 40½"

Bargello for Baby

Over the years, so many quilters have asked me for a bargello-for-baby design. With only 10 fabrics and three strip sets, this little quilt is quick and easy to make. I chose soft pastels, one for a girl and one for a boy. I can even see this stitched in shades of cream for a christening quilt. For a brighter version, see "Gallery of Quilts" on page 76.

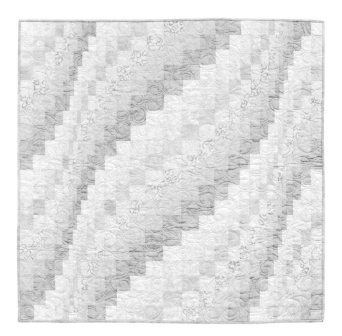

Pieced by author and quilted by Fran Henney of Parksville, British Columbia, Canada

Choosing Fabrics

Select 10 fabrics in one color group with values ranging from light to dark.

Materials

Yardage is based on 42"-wide fabric.

⅓ yard *each* of 10 bargello fabrics
½ yard of dark fabric for binding
2½ yards of fabric for backing
44" x 45" piece of batting

Cutting

From *each* of the 10 bargello fabrics, cut:
3 strips, 2½" x 42"

From the dark fabric for binding, cut:
5 strips, 2¼" x 42"

Fabric Map

Referring to page 8, use a scrap of each bargello fabric to create a fabric map. You'll need to refer to your map throughout the project in order to position all of the strips correctly to make the design shown.

Making the Strip-Set Tubes

To get the length needed for the quilt, two strip sets are sewn together into a single tube. You'll need two 20-fabric tubes; one will be a full-width (42") tube, and the other will be a half-width (21") tube. From these two tubes, you'll be able to cut enough slices for the entire quilt.

1. Referring to "Building Strip Sets" on page 9 and using the 2½"-wide bargello fabric strips, sew the strips together in numerical order according to your fabric map to make three identical strip sets. Press all seam allowances toward the even-numbered fabrics.

2. Join two of the strip sets along their long edges, matching fabric 1 on the first strip set to fabric 10 on the second strip set. Press the seam allowances toward fabric 10.

3. Fold the strip set in half lengthwise, right sides together, carefully matching the two remaining long raw edges to make a tube. Make sure the rectangular unit lies flat and straight and that the tube isn't skewed. Sew along the raw edge using a scant 1/4" seam allowance. Carefully press the seam allowances toward fabric 10 without pressing any other creases in the unit.

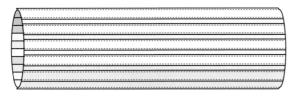

Make 1 full-width tube.

4. Cut the third strip set in half to make two 21"-wide strip units. Repeat steps 2 and 3 to make a half-width tube, 21" wide.

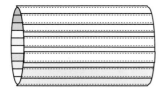

Make 1 half-width tube.

Cutting the Slices

Refer to "Cutting Slices" on page 11 as needed for guidance. Place a tube on a cutting mat and cut a slice for each row in the width indicated on the "Bargello for Baby Design Chart" on page 16.

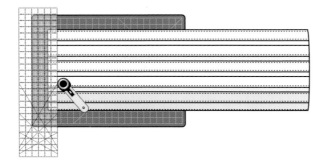

Making the Rows

Lay out the slices in the order indicated on the chart and turn each fabric loop right side out.

1. For row 1, remove the stitching between fabrics 1 and 10. Using your fabric map as a guide, compare your finished row to row 1 on the chart. The numbers assigned to your fabrics should be in the same order as the chart numbers for row 1.

2. For row 2, remove the stitching between fabrics 1 and 2. Using your fabric map as a guide, compare your finished row to row 2 on the chart. Make sure all seam allowances are pressed toward the even-numbered fabrics.

3. Continue working in the same manner, building one row at a time. Referring to your fabric map and using the bold line on the chart as a guide, remove the stitching between segments. After completing each new row, check that it matches the chart and that the seam allowances are pressed toward the even-numbered fabrics.

KEEPING TRACK

You may find it helpful to mark completed rows on your chart with a check mark, or you can cover the completed rows with sticky notes.

Joining the Rows

1. With right sides together and raw edges aligned, place row 2 on top of row 1. Using a scant 1/4"-wide seam allowance, join the rows along their long edges, carefully matching the seam intersections with your fingers. Press the seam allowances toward row 2.

2. Continue in the same manner, sewing the rows in numerical order and pressing the seam allowances toward the newly added row.

3. Finish by basting around the quilt top about 1/8" from the outer edges to stabilize the seams for quilting.

Finishing

For more details on any of the following steps, go to ShopMartingale.com/HowtoQuilt for free downloadable information.

1. Layer the quilt top with batting and backing. Baste and quilt as desired. (Or take the neatly folded quilt top and backing to your professional long-arm machine quilter.)
2. Using the 2¼"-wide binding strips, make and attach the binding.

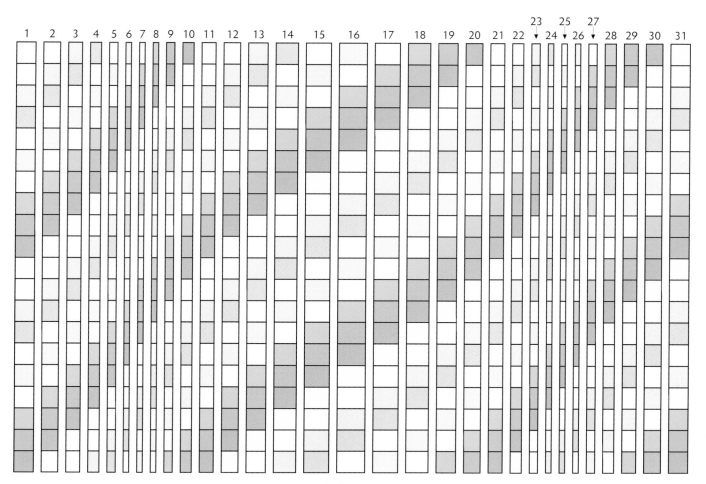

Quilt layout

Row number	1	2	3	4	5	6	7	8	9	10	11	12	13	14	15	16	17	18	19	20	21	22	23	24	25	26	27	28	29	30	31
Cut width of rows	2¼"	2"	1¾"	1½"	1¼"	1"	1"	1"	1¼"	1½"	1¾"	2"	2¼"	2½"	2¾"	3"	2¾"	2½"	2¼"	2"	1¾"	1½"	1¼"	1"	1"	1"	1¼"	1½"	1¾"	2"	2¼"
Fabric number	1	2	3	4	5	6	7	8	9	10	1	2	3	4	5	6	7	8	9	10	1	2	3	4	5	6	7	8	9	10	1
	2	3	4	5	6	7	8	9	10	1	2	3	4	5	6	7	8	9	10	1	2	3	4	5	6	7	8	9	10	1	2
	3	4	5	6	7	8	9	10	1	2	3	4	5	6	7	8	9	10	1	2	3	4	5	6	7	8	9	10	1	2	3
	4	5	6	7	8	9	10	1	2	3	4	5	6	7	8	9	10	1	2	3	4	5	6	7	8	9	10	1	2	3	4
	5	6	7	8	9	10	1	2	3	4	5	6	7	8	9	10	1	2	3	4	5	6	7	8	9	10	1	2	3	4	5
	6	7	8	9	10	1	2	3	4	5	6	7	8	9	10	1	2	3	4	5	6	7	8	9	10	1	2	3	4	5	6
	7	8	9	10	1	2	3	4	5	6	7	8	9	10	1	2	3	4	5	6	7	8	9	10	1	2	3	4	5	6	7
	8	9	10	1	2	3	4	5	6	7	8	9	10	1	2	3	4	5	6	7	8	9	10	1	2	3	4	5	6	7	8
	9	10	1	2	3	4	5	6	7	8	9	10	1	2	3	4	5	6	7	8	9	10	1	2	3	4	5	6	7	8	9
	10	1	2	3	4	5	6	7	8	9	10	1	2	3	4	5	6	7	8	9	10	1	2	3	4	5	6	7	8	9	10
	1	2	3	4	5	6	7	8	9	10	1	2	3	4	5	6	7	8	9	10	1	2	3	4	5	6	7	8	9	10	1
	2	3	4	5	6	7	8	9	10	1	2	3	4	5	6	7	8	9	10	1	2	3	4	5	6	7	8	9	10	1	2
	3	4	5	6	7	8	9	10	1	2	3	4	5	6	7	8	9	10	1	2	3	4	5	6	7	8	9	10	1	2	3
	4	5	6	7	8	9	10	1	2	3	4	5	6	7	8	9	10	1	2	3	4	5	6	7	8	9	10	1	2	3	4
	5	6	7	8	9	10	1	2	3	4	5	6	7	8	9	10	1	2	3	4	5	6	7	8	9	10	1	2	3	4	5
	6	7	8	9	10	1	2	3	4	5	6	7	8	9	10	1	2	3	4	5	6	7	8	9	10	1	2	3	4	5	6
	7	8	9	10	1	2	3	4	5	6	7	8	9	10	1	2	3	4	5	6	7	8	9	10	1	2	3	4	5	6	7
	8	9	10	1	2	3	4	5	6	7	8	9	10	1	2	3	4	5	6	7	8	9	10	1	2	3	4	5	6	7	8
	9	10	1	2	3	4	5	6	7	8	9	10	1	2	3	4	5	6	7	8	9	10	1	2	3	4	5	6	7	8	9
	10	1	2	3	4	5	6	7	8	9	10	1	2	3	4	5	6	7	8	9	10	1	2	3	4	5	6	7	8	9	10

Bargello Bed Runner and Banded Pillowcases

When I was first asked for a bed-runner design, I didn't even know what a bed runner was. Now, I think I need a duvet for the winter so I can show off this project across the foot of my own bed. Instead of making matching pillows, I thought matching pillowcases would be different. I've come to prefer special pillowcases for the extra pillows on my bed.

Choosing Fabrics

This bed set uses 10 fabrics in one color group, with values ranging from light to dark.

Materials

Yardage is based on 42"-wide fabric. Materials are sufficient for making 1 bed runner and 2 pillowcases.

½ yard *each* of 10 bargello fabrics
½ yard of dark fabric for binding
2¼ yards of solid fabric for 2 pillowcases
2⅝ yards of fabric for backing
32" x 84" piece of batting

Cutting

From *each* of the 10 bargello fabrics, cut:*
5 strips, 2½" x 42"

From the dark fabric for binding, cut:
6 strips, 2¼" x 42"

You'll need 4 strips of each fabric for the bed runner and 1 strip of each fabric for the banded pillowcases. Instructions for cutting the solid fabric for the pillowcases can be found in "Making the Pillowcases" on page 23.

Fabric Map

Referring to page 8, use a scrap of each bargello fabric to create a fabric map. You'll need to refer to your map throughout the project in order to position all of the strips correctly to make the design shown.

Making the Strip-Set Tubes

To get the length needed for the bed runner, two strip sets are sewn together into a single tube. You'll need two 20-fabric full-width (42") tubes for the bed runner. The remaining strip set will be used to make a half-width (21") tube for the pillowcases.

1. Referring to "Building Strip Sets" on page 9 and using the 2½"-wide bargello fabric strips, sew the strips together in numerical order according to your fabric map to make five identical strip sets. Press all seam allowances toward the even-numbered fabrics. Set aside one strip set for the "Banded Pillowcases" on page 21.
2. Join two of the strip sets along their long edges, matching fabric 1 on the first strip set to fabric 10 on the second strip set. Press the seam allowances toward fabric 10.

Pieced by author and quilted by Gail Stenberg of Nanaimo, British Columbia, Canada

BED RUNNER FINISHED SIZE: 26½" x 78½"

3. Fold the strip set in half lengthwise, right sides together, carefully matching the two remaining long raw edges to make a tube. Make sure the rectangular unit lies flat and straight and that the tube isn't skewed. Sew along the raw edge using a scant ¼" seam allowance. Carefully press the seam allowances toward fabric 10 without pressing any other creases in the unit. Repeat the process with the remaining two strip sets. Make two full-width tubes.

Make 2 full-width tubes.

Cutting the Slices

Refer to "Cutting Slices" on page 11 as needed for guidance. Place a tube on a cutting mat and cut a slice for each row in the width indicated on the "Bargello Bed Runner Design Chart" on page 20. (Set aside the leftover tube to use for the Banded Pillowcases.)

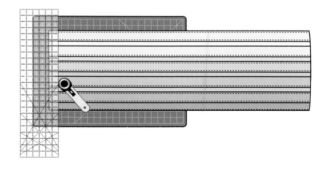

Bottom Half

The bed runner is built in two halves. The bottom half consists of 20 fabrics in each row and the top half has 19 fabrics per row. Both halves are constructed separately and then joined together to complete the bed runner. Lay out the slices in the order indicated on the chart and turn each fabric loop right side out.

1. For row 1, remove the stitching between fabrics 1 and 10. Using your fabric map as a guide, compare your finished row to row 1 on the chart.

The numbers assigned to your fabrics should be in the same order as the chart numbers for row 1.

2. For row 2, remove the stitching between fabrics 9 and 10. Using your fabric map as a guide, compare your finished row to row 2 on the chart. Make sure all seam allowances are pressed toward the even-numbered fabrics.

3. Continue working in the same manner, building one row at a time. Referring to your fabric map and using the bold line on the chart as a guide, remove the stitching between segments. After completing each new row, check that it matches the chart and that the seam allowances are pressed toward the even-numbered fabrics.

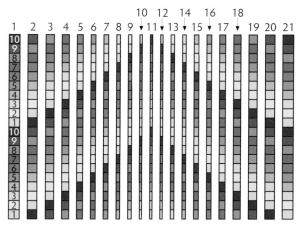

Design layout (bottom half)

Joining the Rows

1. With right sides together and raw edges aligned, place row 2 on top of row 1. Using a scant ¼"-wide seam allowance, join the rows along their long edges, carefully matching the seam intersections with your fingers. Press the seam allowances toward row 2.

2. Continue in the same manner, sewing the rows in numerical order and pressing the seam allowances toward the newly added row.

Top Half

Referring to your fabric map, cut slices as required in the width indicated on the chart. Working in the same manner as before and using the bold line on the chart as a guide, remove the stitching between segments.

Remove and discard the segment at the bottom of each row. After completing each new row, check that it matches the chart and that the seam allowances are pressed toward the even-numbered fabrics. Then join the rows together as you did for the bottom half.

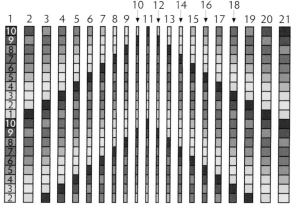

Design layout (top half)

Assembly

1. Rotate the top half 180° and check to ensure that it's a mirror image of the bottom half of the bed runner. The seam allowances should be going in opposite directions and nesting together. Carefully pin the two halves together, matching the seam intersections.

2. Use a scant ¼"-wide seam allowance to stitch the two halves together. Press the seam allowances open.

3. Finish by basting around the bed-runner top about ⅛" from the outer edges to stabilize the seams for quilting.

Finishing

For more details on any of the following steps, go to ShopMartingale.com/HowtoQuilt for free downloadable information.

1. Layer the bed-runner top with batting and backing. Baste and quilt as desired. (Or take the neatly folded bed-runner top and backing to your professional long-arm machine quilter.)

2. Using the 2¼"-wide binding strips, make and attach the binding.

BARGELLO BED RUNNER DESIGN CHART

Bottom half of the bed runner

Row number	1	2	3	4	5	6	7	8	9	10	11	12	13	14	15	16	17	18	19	20	21
Cut width of rows	2¾"	2½"	2¼"	2"	1¾"	1½"	1½"	1¼"	1¼"	1"	1"	1"	1¼"	1¼"	1½"	1½"	1¾"	2"	2¼"	2½"	2¾"
Fabric number	10	9	8	7	6	5	4	3	2	1	10	1	2	3	4	5	6	7	8	9	10
	9	8	7	6	5	4	3	2	1	10	9	10	1	2	3	4	5	6	7	8	9
	8	7	6	5	4	3	2	1	10	9	8	9	10	1	2	3	4	5	6	7	8
	7	6	5	4	3	2	1	10	9	8	7	8	9	10	1	2	3	4	5	6	7
	6	5	4	3	2	1	10	9	8	7	6	7	8	9	10	1	2	3	4	5	6
	5	4	3	2	1	10	9	8	7	6	5	6	7	8	9	10	1	2	3	4	5
	4	3	2	1	10	9	8	7	6	5	4	5	6	7	8	9	10	1	2	3	4
	3	2	1	10	9	8	7	6	5	4	3	4	5	6	7	8	9	10	1	2	3
	2	1	10	9	8	7	6	5	4	3	2	3	4	5	6	7	8	9	10	1	2
	1	10	9	8	7	6	5	4	3	2	1	2	3	4	5	6	7	8	9	10	1
	10	9	8	7	6	5	4	3	2	1	10	1	2	3	4	5	6	7	8	9	10
	9	8	7	6	5	4	3	2	1	10	9	10	1	2	3	4	5	6	7	8	9
	8	7	6	5	4	3	2	1	10	9	8	9	10	1	2	3	4	5	6	7	8
	7	6	5	4	3	2	1	10	9	8	7	8	9	10	1	2	3	4	5	6	7
	6	5	4	3	2	1	10	9	8	7	6	7	8	9	10	1	2	3	4	5	6
	5	4	3	2	1	10	9	8	7	6	5	6	7	8	9	10	1	2	3	4	5
	4	3	2	1	10	9	8	7	6	5	4	5	6	7	8	9	10	1	2	3	4
	3	2	1	10	9	8	7	6	5	4	3	4	5	6	7	8	9	10	1	2	3
	2	1	10	9	8	7	6	5	4	3	2	3	4	5	6	7	8	9	10	1	2
	1	10	9	8	7	6	5	4	3	2	1	2	3	4	5	6	7	8	9	10	1

BARGELLO BED RUNNER DESIGN CHART

Top half of the bed runner

Row number	1	2	3	4	5	6	7	8	9	10	11	12	13	14	15	16	17	18	19	20	21
Cut width of rows	2¾"	2½"	2¼"	2"	1¾"	1½"	1½"	1¼"	1¼"	1"	1"	1"	1¼"	1¼"	1½"	1½"	1¾"	2"	2¼"	2½"	2¾"
Fabric number	10	9	8	7	6	5	4	3	2	1	10	1	2	3	4	5	6	7	8	9	10
	9	8	7	6	5	4	3	2	1	10	9	10	1	2	3	4	5	6	7	8	9
	8	7	6	5	4	3	2	1	10	9	8	9	10	1	2	3	4	5	6	7	8
	7	6	5	4	3	2	1	10	9	8	7	8	9	10	1	2	3	4	5	6	7
	6	5	4	3	2	1	10	9	8	7	6	7	8	9	10	1	2	3	4	5	6
	5	4	3	2	1	10	9	8	7	6	5	6	7	8	9	10	1	2	3	4	5
	4	3	2	1	10	9	8	7	6	5	4	5	6	7	8	9	10	1	2	3	4
	3	2	1	10	9	8	7	6	5	4	3	4	5	6	7	8	9	10	1	2	3
	2	1	10	9	8	7	6	5	4	3	2	3	4	5	6	7	8	9	10	1	2
	1	10	9	8	7	6	5	4	3	2	1	2	3	4	5	6	7	8	9	10	1
	10	9	8	7	6	5	4	3	2	1	10	1	2	3	4	5	6	7	8	9	10
	9	8	7	6	5	4	3	2	1	10	9	10	1	2	3	4	5	6	7	8	9
	8	7	6	5	4	3	2	1	10	9	8	9	10	1	2	3	4	5	6	7	8
	7	6	5	4	3	2	1	10	9	8	7	8	9	10	1	2	3	4	5	6	7
	6	5	4	3	2	1	10	9	8	7	6	7	8	9	10	1	2	3	4	5	6
	5	4	3	2	1	10	9	8	7	6	5	6	7	8	9	10	1	2	3	4	5
	4	3	2	1	10	9	8	7	6	5	4	5	6	7	8	9	10	1	2	3	4
	3	2	1	10	9	8	7	6	5	4	3	4	5	6	7	8	9	10	1	2	3
	2	1	10	9	8	7	6	5	4	3	2	3	4	5	6	7	8	9	10	1	2

Pieced by author

PILLOWCASE FINISHED SIZE: 20" x 32"

Banded Pillowcases

For the two banded pillowcases, you'll need the remaining strip set of bargello fabrics and the leftover strip-set tube from the bed runner. You'll also need the 2¼ yards of solid fabric.

Making the Strip-Set Tube

1. Using the remaining strip set from step 1 of "Making the Strip-Set Tubes" on page 17, cut the strip set in half to make two 21"-wide strip units. Join the two strip units along their long edges, matching fabric 1 on the first strip unit to fabric 10 on the second strip unit. Press the seam allowances toward fabric 10.

2. Fold the strip unit in half lengthwise, right sides together, carefully matching the two remaining long raw edges to make a tube. Make sure the rectangular unit lies flat and straight and that the tube isn't skewed. Sew along the raw edge using a scant ¼" seam allowance to make a half-width tube, 21" wide. Carefully press the seam allowances toward fabric 10 without pressing any other creases in the unit.

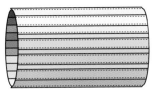

Make 1 half-width tube.

Cutting the Slices

Refer to "Cutting Slices" on page 11 as needed for guidance. Place a tube on a cutting mat and cut a slice for each row in the width indicated on the "Banded Pillowcases Design Chart" on page 24. Repeat to cut a second slice for each row in the width indicated on the chart for the second pillowcase band.

Making the Rows

Directions are for making one band. Repeat to make a second band. Lay out the slices in the order indicated on the chart and turn each fabric loop right side out.

1. For row 1, remove the stitching between fabrics 4 and 5. Using your fabric map as a guide, compare your finished row to row 1 on the chart. The numbers assigned to your fabrics should be in the same order as the chart numbers for row 1.
2. For row 2, remove the stitching between fabrics 3 and 4. Using your fabric map as a guide, compare your finished row to row 2 on the chart. Make sure all seam allowances are pressed toward the even-numbered fabrics.
3. Continue working in the same manner, building one row at a time. Referring to your fabric map and using the bold line on the chart as a guide, remove the stitching between segments. After completing each new row, check that it matches the chart and that the seam allowances are pressed toward the even-numbered fabrics.

Joining the Rows

1. With right sides together and raw edges aligned, place row 2 on top of row 1. Using a scant ¼"-wide seam allowance, join the rows along their long edges, carefully matching the seam intersections with your fingers. Press the seam allowances toward row 2.

2. Continue in the same manner, sewing the rows in numerical order and pressing the seam allowances toward the newly added row to complete one bargello band.

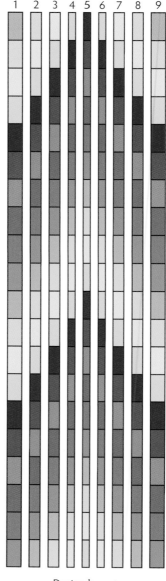

Design layout

3. Repeat steps 1 and 2 to make a second bargello band, sewing from the right side of the chart (row 9) working toward the left side (row 1) to create a mirror-image band.

Making the Pillowcases

1. Measure the width of each bargello band; they should each be 7" wide. From the solid fabric for the pillowcases, cut two 7" x 42" strips.

2. Center a bargello band on each solid-fabric band, right sides together, so that the bargello bands are a mirror-image of each other. Trim each solid-fabric band to the same length as the bargello band. Then stitch along the long bottom edge of each bargello band using a ¼"-wide seam allowance, making sure to maintain the mirror image.

3. Flip the bands open, right sides up, and press the seam allowances toward the solid-fabric band. Then fold each band, wrong sides together, along the seam line, making sure the solid-fabric band is hidden beneath the bargello band. Press the length of each band. Open each band again, and refold it in half, right sides together; align the seams along the short ends and pin in place. On each band, sew the ends together using a ¼"-wide seam allowance. Press the seam allowances open.

4. Fold each band along the creased seam line between the bargello and solid fabric, wrong sides together, and align the raw edges to make a lined tube of bargello. Your second tube should be a mirror-image of the first tube.

5. Measure the width of your folded flat bargello tube; it should be 20". Cut two 27" x 42" pieces of solid fabric. Fold each piece in half, wrong sides together, to make two 21" x 27" pieces. Measuring from the fold, trim each piece to 20½" (or the measurement of your folded band plus ½"). Keep each piece folded with wrong sides together.

6. To make a French seam, on each folded solid piece from step 5, sew along the long raw edge using a ⅛"-wide seam allowance to make a 27"-long tube.

7. Turn each tube wrong side out and press it flat along the seam line. Fold each tube, right side together, along the newly stitched seam and sew ¼" from the folded edge to enclose the first seam. This completes the French seam along one side on each pillowcase tube.

8. Place a bargello tube and a pillowcase tube, right sides together, with the seam aligned and the raw edges matching. Pin in place and stitch using a ¼"-wide seam allowance.

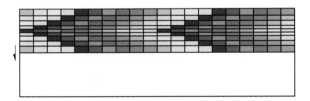

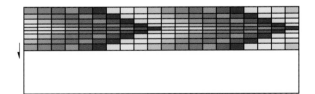

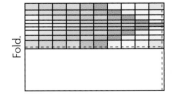

9. Turn the pillowcase tube inside out so the wrong side is inside the bargello tube with the pillowcase tube folded over the edge of the seam allowance. Press along the fold. With the bargello side facing up and using invisible thread in the top of your machine, stitch in the ditch along the bargello seam line. This creates a ¼"- to ⅜"-wide tuck on the right side of your pillowcase below the bargello band. Repeat the process with the second bargello band and pillowcase tube.

10. Turn the entire pillowcase right side out again. With wrong sides together and raw edges aligned, start at the side seam and sew across the bottom of the pillowcase using a ⅛"-wide seam allowance. Turn the pillowcase wrong side out and press along the seam line. Sew ¼" from the folded edge to enclose the first seam and complete the French seam along the bottom of the pillowcase. Finish by turning the pillowcase right side out and pressing the edge of each seam and the tuck so they're nice and flat. Repeat to make a French seam along the bottom of the second pillowcase.

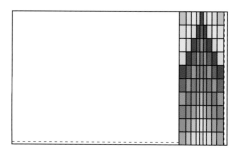

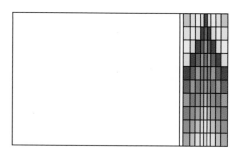

BANDED PILLOWCASES DESIGN CHART									
Row number	1	2	3	4	5	6	7	8	9
Cut width of rows	1½"	1¼"	1¼"	1"	1"	1"	1¼"	1¼"	1½"
Fabric number	4	3	2	1	10	1	2	3	4
	3	2	1	10	9	10	1	2	3
	2	1	10	9	8	9	10	1	2
	1	10	9	8	7	8	9	10	1
	10	9	8	7	6	7	8	9	10
	9	8	7	6	5	6	7	8	9
	8	7	6	5	4	5	6	7	8
	7	6	5	4	3	4	5	6	7
	6	5	4	3	2	3	4	5	6
	5	4	3	2	1	2	3	4	5
	4	3	2	1	10	1	2	3	4
	3	2	1	10	9	10	1	2	3
	2	1	10	9	8	9	10	1	2
	1	10	9	8	7	8	9	10	1
	10	9	8	7	6	7	8	9	10
	9	8	7	6	5	6	7	8	9
	8	7	6	5	4	5	6	7	8
	7	6	5	4	3	4	5	6	7
	6	5	4	3	2	3	4	5	6
	5	4	3	2	1	2	3	4	5

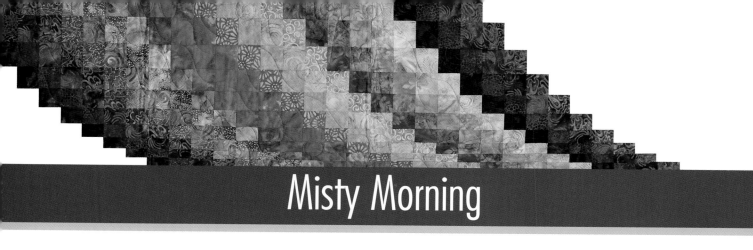

Misty Morning

"Misty Morning" is reminiscent of the early morning sun rising through the swirls of mist over the ocean, which was my view from the deck at my Nanaimo condo. I'm so glad I captured and framed so many of the amazing ocean shots from that place. Now I live ground level in Parksville with an entirely different natural beauty.

Choosing Fabric

This quilt uses 20 fabrics in two color groups: blue and hot pink. I used five blue tone-on-tone fabrics, seven hot-pink blending into red fabrics, and eight blue fabrics with obvious hot-pink/red tones blended in. The fabrics in each group should range in value from light to dark.

Materials

Yardage is based on 42"-wide fabric.

½ yard *each* of 20 bargello fabrics
⅝ yard of dark fabric for binding
3⅞ yards of fabric for backing
66" x 86" piece of batting

Cutting

From *each* of the 20 bargello fabrics cut:
5 strips, 2½" x 42"

From the dark fabric for binding cut:
8 strips, 2¼" x 42"

Fabric Map

Referring to page 8, use a scrap of each of your bargello fabrics to create a fabric map. You'll need to refer to your map throughout the project in order to position all of the strips correctly to make the design shown.

Making the Strip Sets

Referring to "Building Strip Sets" on page 9, and using the 2½"-wide bargello fabric strips, sew the strips together in numerical order according to your fabric map to build five identical strip sets. Press all seam allowances toward the even-numbered fabric strips.

Fabric 1
Fabric 2
Fabric 3
Fabric 4
Fabric 5
Fabric 6
Fabric 7
Fabric 8
Fabric 9
Fabric 10
Fabric 11
Fabric 12
Fabric 13
Fabric 14
Fabric 15
Fabric 16
Fabric 17
Fabric 18
Fabric 19
Fabric 20

Make 5 strip sets.

Pieced by author and machine quilted by Nadia Wilson, Port Hardy, British Columbia, Canada

FINISHED SIZE: 61" x 80½"

Row 1

1. Referring to "Cutting Slices" on page 11, cut two 2¾"-wide slices from a strip set.
2. Sew fabric 1 of the first slice to fabric 20 of the second slice. Press the seam allowances toward row 20. This completes row 1.
3. Using your fabric map as a guide, compare your finished row to row 1 on the "Misty Morning Design Chart" on page 28. The numbers assigned to your fabrics should be in the same order as the chart numbers for row 1.

Row 2

1. From a strip set, cut two 2½"-wide slices.
2. Sew fabric 1 on the first slice to fabric 20 on the second slice. Then sew the ends (fabrics 1 and 20) together to make a loop. Press both seam allowances toward fabric 20.

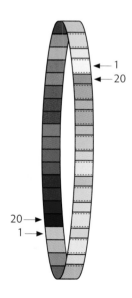

3. Turn the fabric loop right side out. Remove the stitching between fabric 1 and fabric 2. Using your fabric map as a guide, compare your

finished row to row 2 on the chart. The numbers assigned to your fabrics should be in the same order as the chart numbers for row 2.

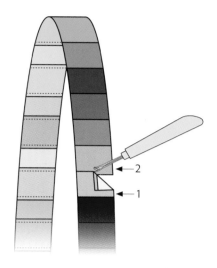

Joining the Rows

With right sides together and raw edges aligned, place row 2 on top of row 1. Using a scant ¼" seam allowance, join the rows along their long edges, carefully matching the seam intersections with your finger. You may want to use a stylus or an awl to hold the seam intersections in place, gently easing the fabric as needed to align the seams. Press the seam allowances toward row 2, and then toward each newly added subsequent row.

Working from the Chart

1. Continue working in the same manner, cutting two slices in the width indicated on the chart and building one row at a time. Referring to your fabric map and using the bold lines on the chart as a guide, remove the stitching between segments as needed and join the segments in the order indicated for the row you're making. Once you've completed 10 rows, you might want to begin a new section with rows 11–20; then build two additional sections for rows 21–30 and rows 31–41. Dividing the project into four sections makes it easier to handle.

MISTY MORNING DESIGN CHART

Row number	1	2	3	4	5	6	7	8	9	10	11	12	13	14	15	16	17	18	19	20	21
Cut width of rows	2¾"	2½"	2¼"	2"	1¾"	1½"	1¼"	1¼"	1"	1"	1¼"	1¼"	1½"	1¾"	2"	2¼"	2½"	2¾"	3"	3¼"	3½"
Fabric number	1	2	3	4	5	6	7	8	9	10	11	12	13	14	15	16	17	18	19	20	1
	2	3	4	5	6	7	8	9	10	11	12	13	14	15	16	17	18	19	20	1	2
	3	4	5	6	7	8	9	10	11	12	13	14	15	16	17	18	19	20	1	2	3
	4	5	6	7	8	9	10	11	12	13	14	15	16	17	18	19	20	1	2	3	4
	5	6	7	8	9	10	11	12	13	14	15	16	17	18	19	20	1	2	3	4	5
	6	7	8	9	10	11	12	13	14	15	16	17	18	19	20	1	2	3	4	5	6
	7	8	9	10	11	12	13	14	15	16	17	18	19	20	1	2	3	4	5	6	7
	8	9	10	11	12	13	14	15	16	17	18	19	20	1	2	3	4	5	6	7	8
	9	10	11	12	13	14	15	16	17	18	19	20	1	2	3	4	5	6	7	8	9
	10	11	12	13	14	15	16	17	18	19	20	1	2	3	4	5	6	7	8	9	10
	11	12	13	14	15	16	17	18	19	20	1	2	3	4	5	6	7	8	9	10	11
	12	13	14	15	16	17	18	19	20	1	2	3	4	5	6	7	8	9	10	11	12
	13	14	15	16	17	18	19	20	1	2	3	4	5	6	7	8	9	10	11	12	13
	14	15	16	17	18	19	20	1	2	3	4	5	6	7	8	9	10	11	12	13	14
	15	16	17	18	19	20	1	2	3	4	5	6	7	8	9	10	11	12	13	14	15
	16	17	18	19	20	1	2	3	4	5	6	7	8	9	10	11	12	13	14	15	16
	17	18	19	20	1	2	3	4	5	6	7	8	9	10	11	12	13	14	15	16	17
	18	19	20	1	2	3	4	5	6	7	8	9	10	11	12	13	14	15	16	17	18
	19	20	1	2	3	4	5	6	7	8	9	10	11	12	13	14	15	16	17	18	19
	20	1	2	3	4	5	6	7	8	9	10	11	12	13	14	15	16	17	18	19	20
	1	2	3	4	5	6	7	8	9	10	11	12	13	14	15	16	17	18	19	20	1
	2	3	4	5	6	7	8	9	10	11	12	13	14	15	16	17	18	19	20	1	2
	3	4	5	6	7	8	9	10	11	12	13	14	15	16	17	18	19	20	1	2	3
	4	5	6	7	8	9	10	11	12	13	14	15	16	17	18	19	20	1	2	3	4
	5	6	7	8	9	10	11	12	13	14	15	16	17	18	19	20	1	2	3	4	5
	6	7	8	9	10	11	12	13	14	15	16	17	18	19	20	1	2	3	4	5	6
	7	8	9	10	11	12	13	14	15	16	17	18	19	20	1	2	3	4	5	6	7
	8	9	10	11	12	13	14	15	16	17	18	19	20	1	2	3	4	5	6	7	8
	9	10	11	12	13	14	15	16	17	18	19	20	1	2	3	4	5	6	7	8	9
	10	11	12	13	14	15	16	17	18	19	20	1	2	3	4	5	6	7	8	9	10
	11	12	13	14	15	16	17	18	19	20	1	2	3	4	5	6	7	8	9	10	11
	12	13	14	15	16	17	18	19	20	1	2	3	4	5	6	7	8	9	10	11	12
	13	14	15	16	17	18	19	20	1	2	3	4	5	6	7	8	9	10	11	12	13
	14	15	16	17	18	19	20	1	2	3	4	5	6	7	8	9	10	11	12	13	14
	15	16	17	18	19	20	1	2	3	4	5	6	7	8	9	10	11	12	13	14	15
	16	17	18	19	20	1	2	3	4	5	6	7	8	9	10	11	12	13	14	15	16
	17	18	19	20	1	2	3	4	5	6	7	8	9	10	11	12	13	14	15	16	17
	18	19	20	1	2	3	4	5	6	7	8	9	10	11	12	13	14	15	16	17	18
	19	20	1	2	3	4	5	6	7	8	9	10	11	12	13	14	15	16	17	18	19
	20	1	2	3	4	5	6	7	8	9	10	11	12	13	14	15	16	17	18	19	20

Row number	22	23	24	25	26	27	28	29	30	31	32	33	34	35	36	37	38	39	40	41
Cut width of rows	3¼"	3"	2¾"	2½"	2¼"	2"	1¾"	1½"	1¼"	1¼"	1"	1"	1¼"	1¼"	1½"	1¾"	2"	2¼"	2½"	2¾"
Fabric number	2	3	4	5	6	7	8	9	10	11	12	13	14	15	16	17	18	19	20	1
	3	4	5	6	7	8	9	10	11	12	13	14	15	16	17	18	19	20	1	2
	4	5	6	7	8	9	10	11	12	13	14	15	16	17	18	19	20	1	2	3
	5	6	7	8	9	10	11	12	13	14	15	16	17	18	19	20	1	2	3	4
	6	7	8	9	10	11	12	13	14	15	16	17	18	19	20	1	2	3	4	5
	7	8	9	10	11	12	13	14	15	16	17	18	19	20	1	2	3	4	5	6
	8	9	10	11	12	13	14	15	16	17	18	19	20	1	2	3	4	5	6	7
	9	10	11	12	13	14	15	16	17	18	19	20	1	2	3	4	5	6	7	8
	10	11	12	13	14	15	16	17	18	19	20	1	2	3	4	5	6	7	8	9
	11	12	13	14	15	16	17	18	19	20	1	2	3	4	5	6	7	8	9	10
	12	13	14	15	16	17	18	19	20	1	2	3	4	5	6	7	8	9	10	11
	13	14	15	16	17	18	19	20	1	2	3	4	5	6	7	8	9	10	11	12
	14	15	16	17	18	19	20	1	2	3	4	5	6	7	8	9	10	11	12	13
	15	16	17	18	19	20	1	2	3	4	5	6	7	8	9	10	11	12	13	14
	16	17	18	19	20	1	2	3	4	5	6	7	8	9	10	11	12	13	14	15
	17	18	19	20	1	2	3	4	5	6	7	8	9	10	11	12	13	14	15	16
	18	19	20	1	2	3	4	5	6	7	8	9	10	11	12	13	14	15	16	17
	19	20	1	2	3	4	5	6	7	8	9	10	11	12	13	14	15	16	17	18
	20	1	2	3	4	5	6	7	8	9	10	11	12	13	14	15	16	17	18	19
	1	2	3	4	5	6	7	8	9	10	11	12	13	14	15	16	17	18	19	20
	2	3	4	5	6	7	8	9	10	11	12	13	14	15	16	17	18	19	20	1
	3	4	5	6	7	8	9	10	11	12	13	14	15	16	17	18	19	20	1	2
	4	5	6	7	8	9	10	11	12	13	14	15	16	17	18	19	20	1	2	3
	5	6	7	8	9	10	11	12	13	14	15	16	17	18	19	20	1	2	3	4
	6	7	8	9	10	11	12	13	14	15	16	17	18	19	20	1	2	3	4	5
	7	8	9	10	11	12	13	14	15	16	17	18	19	20	1	2	3	4	5	6
	8	9	10	11	12	13	14	15	16	17	18	19	20	1	2	3	4	5	6	7
	9	10	11	12	13	14	15	16	17	18	19	20	1	2	3	4	5	6	7	8
	10	11	12	13	14	15	16	17	18	19	20	1	2	3	4	5	6	7	8	9
	11	12	13	14	15	16	17	18	19	20	1	2	3	4	5	6	7	8	9	10
	12	13	14	15	16	17	18	19	20	1	2	3	4	5	6	7	8	9	10	11
	13	14	15	16	17	18	19	20	1	2	3	4	5	6	7	8	9	10	11	12
	14	15	16	17	18	19	20	1	2	3	4	5	6	7	8	9	10	11	12	13
	15	16	17	18	19	20	1	2	3	4	5	6	7	8	9	10	11	12	13	14
	16	17	18	19	20	1	2	3	4	5	6	7	8	9	10	11	12	13	14	15
	17	18	19	20	1	2	3	4	5	6	7	8	9	10	11	12	13	14	15	16
	18	19	20	1	2	3	4	5	6	7	8	9	10	11	12	13	14	15	16	17
	19	20	1	2	3	4	5	6	7	8	9	10	11	12	13	14	15	16	17	18
	20	1	2	3	4	5	6	7	8	9	10	11	12	13	14	15	16	17	18	19
	1	2	3	4	5	6	7	8	9	10	11	12	13	14	15	16	17	18	19	20

2. After completing each new row, check that it matches the chart and that the seam allowances are pressed toward the even-numbered fabrics.
3. Join each new row to the section you're constructing and press the seam allowances toward the newly added row.

Assembly

1. Join the four sections in the correct numerical order to complete your quilt top. Press all the same allowances in the same direction.
2. Once all the sections are sewn together, finish by basting around the quilt top about 1/8" from the outer edges to stabilize the seams for quilting.

Finishing

For more details on any of the following steps, go to ShopMartingale.com/HowtoQuilt for free downloadable information.

1. Layer the quilt top with batting and backing. Baste and quilt as desired. (Or take the neatly folded quilt top and backing to your professional long-arm machine quilter.)
2. Using the 2¼"-wide binding strips, make and attach the binding.

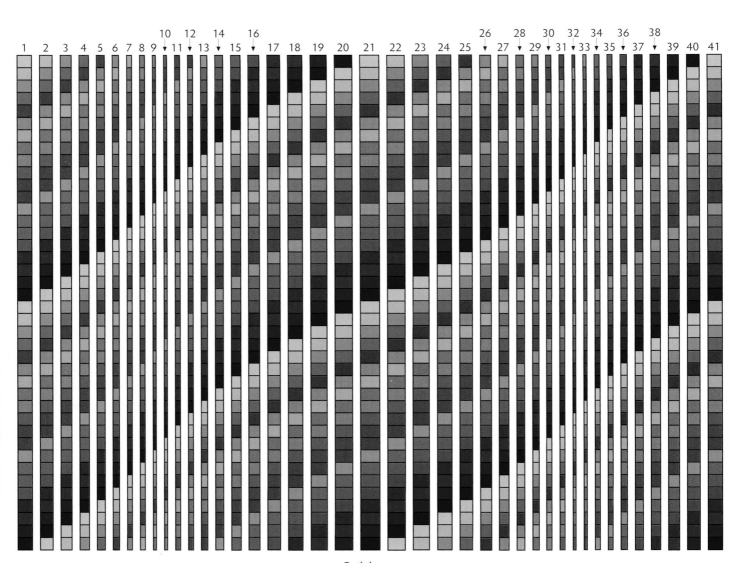

Quilt layout

Love Song

"Love Song" fulfills a number of requests I've had from quilters. It's a black-and-white quilt made from fat quarters and finishes much smaller than the quilts I usually make. A touch of appliqué nails down the theme. It probably isn't small enough to suit some quilters but I prefer making larger quilts, so this one was a challenge for me to execute.

Choosing Fabric

This quilt uses 20 fat quarters in two color groups: 9 in one color group (white on black) and 11 in another color group (black with white). Fabrics in each color group should range from light to dark and include one or two large-scale fabrics. Think about using as many music theme fabrics as possible.

Materials

Yardage is based on 42"-wide fabric. Fat quarters measure 18" x 21".

20 fat quarters for bargello
⅓ yard of dark fabric for binding
7" x 7" square of red fabric for appliqué
1 yard of fabric for backing
36" x 36" piece of batting
6½" x 6½" square of fusible web

Cutting

From *each* of the 20 fat quarters, cut:
5 strips, 1¼" x 21"

From the dark binding fabric, cut:
4 strips, 2¼" x 42"

Fabric Map

Referring to page 8, use a scrap of each of your bargello fabrics to create a fabric map. You'll need to refer to your map throughout the project in order to position all of your strips correctly to make the design shown. For the quilt on page 32, fabric 1 is the lightest white fabric and fabric 20 is the darkest black.

Making the Strip-Set Tubes

To achieve the length needed for the quilt, two strip sets are sewn together into a single tube. You'll need three 20-fabric tubes; two will be full-width (21") tubes, and the other will be a half-width (10") tube.

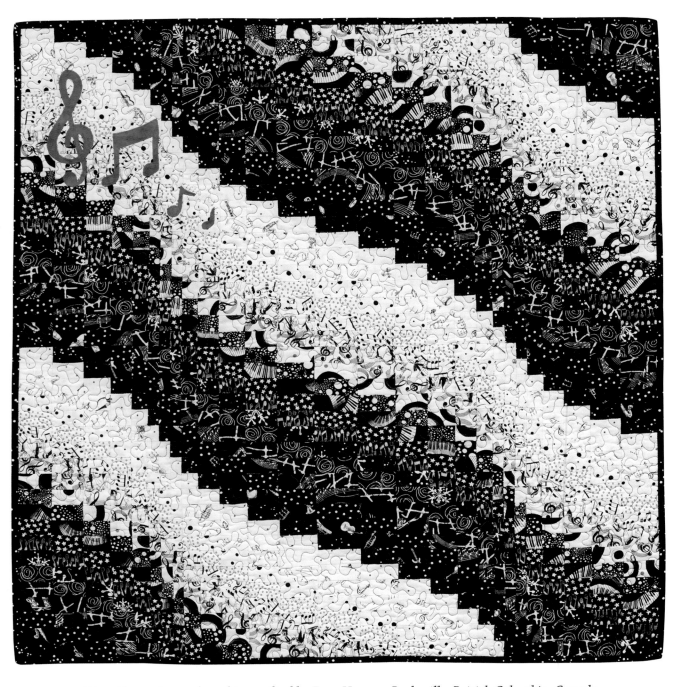

Pieced by author and machine quilted by Fran Henney, Parksville, British Columbia, Canada
FINISHED SIZE: 30½" x 30½"

Love Song

1. Referring to "Building Strip Sets" on page 9 and using the 1¼"-wide bargello fabric strips, sew the strips together in numerical order according to your fabric map to make five identical strip sets. Press all seam allowances toward the even-numbered fabric.

Fabric 1
Fabric 2
Fabric 3
Fabric 4
Fabric 5
Fabric 6
Fabric 7
Fabric 8
Fabric 9
Fabric 10
Fabric 11
Fabric 12
Fabric 13
Fabric 14
Fabric 15
Fabric 16
Fabric 17
Fabric 18
Fabric 19
Fabric 20

Make 5 strip sets.

2. Join two of the strip sets together along their long edges, matching fabric 1 on the first strip set to fabric 20 on the second strip set. Press the seam allowances toward fabric 20.

3. Fold the strip in half lengthwise, right sides together, carefully matching the two remaining long raw edges to make a tube. Make sure the rectangular unit lies flat and straight and that the tube isn't skewed. Sew along the raw edge using a scant ¼"-wide seam allowance. Carefully press the seam allowances toward fabric 20 without pressing any other creases in the unit. Repeat the process to make a second full-width tube.

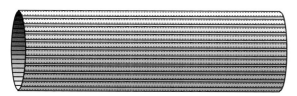

Make 2 full-width tubes.

4. Cut the last strip set in half to make two 10"-wide strip sets. Repeat steps 2 and 3 to make a half-width tube, 10" wide.

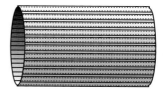

Make 1 half-width tube.

WRONG SIDES OUT

By keeping the strip-set tubes wrong sides out, the tubes will lie flat on your cutting surface and be easier to cut into slices.

Cutting the Slices

Refer to "Cutting Slices" on page 11 as needed for guidance. Place a tube on a cutting mat and cut a slice for each row in the width indicated on the "Love Song Design Chart" on page 36.

Making the Rows

Start on the far left with row 1 and work to row 27 on the far right. Lay out the slices in the order indicated on the chart and turn each fabric loop right side out.

1. For row 1, remove the stitching between fabrics 1 and 20. Using your fabric map as a guide, compare your finished row to row 1 on the chart. The numbers assigned to your fabrics should be in the same order as the chart numbers for row 1.

2. For row 2, remove the stitching between fabrics 19 and 20. Using your fabric map as a guide, compare your finished row to row 2 on the chart. Make sure all seam allowances are pressed toward the even-numbered fabrics.

CORRECT POSITION

Always make sure your loop is positioned correctly with fabric 1 at the top and fabric 20 at the bottom before you remove the necessary stitching. It's easy to get the strip upside down until you get the hang of working with the pieced loops.

3. Continue working in the same manner, building one row at a time. Referring to your fabric map and using the bold line on the chart as a guide, remove the stitching between segments. After completing each new row, check that it matches the chart and that the seam allowances are pressed toward the even-numbered fabrics.

Joining the Rows

1. With right sides together and raw edges aligned, place row 2 on top of row 1. Using a scant ¼"-wide seam allowance, join the rows along their long edges, carefully matching the seam intersections with your fingers. Press the seam allowances toward row 2.

2. Continue in the same manner, sewing the rows in numerical order and pressing the seam allowances toward the newly added row.

3. Finish by basting around the quilt top about ⅛" from the outer edges to stabilize the seams for quilting.

DESIGN WALL

If you have a large design wall, I recommend making a few rows and pinning them to your design wall as you go. Then sew the rows together, pressing the seam allowances after adding each row. That way you'll have a preview of your quilt before it's finished, and the final assembly seems to go a bit faster.

Appliqué

1. Following the manufacturer's instructions, trace the patterns, below and opposite, onto the paper side of the fusible web. You'll need one of each shape. Fuse the shapes to the wrong side of the red square. Cut out the shapes on the drawn line.

2. Arrange and fuse the shapes on the quilt top as shown in the photo on page 32. With matching thread, stitch around each shape using a blanket stitch. You can also use a zigzag stitch or other decorative stitch on your machine if you prefer.

Finishing

For more details on any of the following steps, go to ShopMartingale.com/HowtoQuilt for free download-able information.

1. Layer the quilt top with batting and backing. Baste and quilt as desired. (Or take the neatly folded quilt top and backing to your professional long-arm machine quilter.)

2. Using the 2¼"-wide binding strips, make and attach the binding.

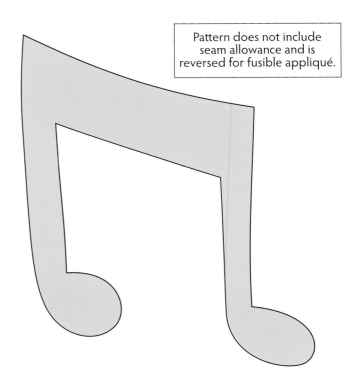

Pattern does not include seam allowance and is reversed for fusible appliqué.

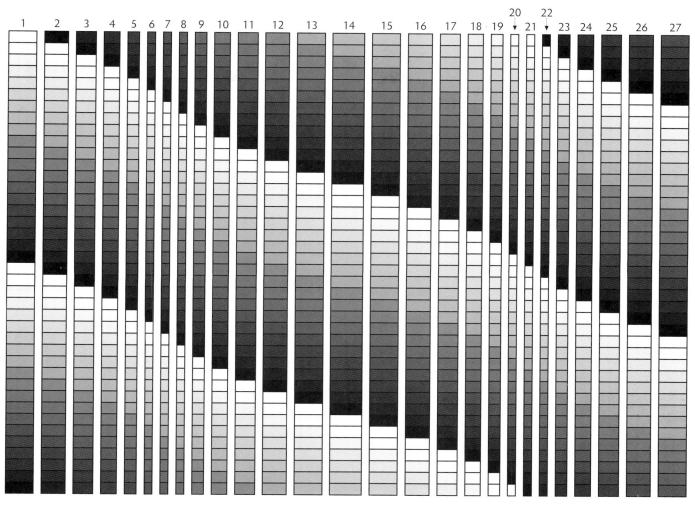

Quilt layout

Row number	1	2	3	4	5	6	7	8	9	10	11	12	13	14	15	16	17	18	19	20	21	22	23	24	25	26	27
Cut width of rows	2¼"	2"	1¾"	1½"	1¼"	1"	1"	1"	1¼"	1½"	1¾"	2"	2¼"	2½"	2¼"	2"	1¾"	1½"	1¼"	1"	1"	1"	1¼"	1½"	1¾"	2"	2¼"
Fabric number 1	1	20	19	18	17	16	15	14	13	12	11	10	9	8	7	6	5	4	3	2	1	20	19	18	17	16	15
2	2	1	20	19	18	17	16	15	14	13	12	11	10	9	8	7	6	5	4	3	2	1	20	19	18	17	16
3	3	2	1	20	19	18	17	16	15	14	13	12	11	10	9	8	7	6	5	4	3	2	1	20	19	18	17
4	4	3	2	1	20	19	18	17	16	15	14	13	12	11	10	9	8	7	6	5	4	3	2	1	20	19	18
5	5	4	3	2	1	20	19	18	17	16	15	14	13	12	11	10	9	8	7	6	5	4	3	2	1	20	19
6	6	5	4	3	2	1	20	19	18	17	16	15	14	13	12	11	10	9	8	7	6	5	4	3	2	1	20
7	7	6	5	4	3	2	1	20	19	18	17	16	15	14	13	12	11	10	9	8	7	6	5	4	3	2	1
8	8	7	6	5	4	3	2	1	20	19	18	17	16	15	14	13	12	11	10	9	8	7	6	5	4	3	2
9	9	8	7	6	5	4	3	2	1	20	19	18	17	16	15	14	13	12	11	10	9	8	7	6	5	4	3
10	10	9	8	7	6	5	4	3	2	1	20	19	18	17	16	15	14	13	12	11	10	9	8	7	6	5	4
11	11	10	9	8	7	6	5	4	3	2	1	20	19	18	17	16	15	14	13	12	11	10	9	8	7	6	5
12	12	11	10	9	8	7	6	5	4	3	2	1	20	19	18	17	16	15	14	13	12	11	10	9	8	7	6
13	13	12	11	10	9	8	7	6	5	4	3	2	1	20	19	18	17	16	15	14	13	12	11	10	9	8	7
14	14	13	12	11	10	9	8	7	6	5	4	3	2	1	20	19	18	17	16	15	14	13	12	11	10	9	8
15	15	14	13	12	11	10	9	8	7	6	5	4	3	2	1	20	19	18	17	16	15	14	13	12	11	10	9
16	16	15	14	13	12	11	10	9	8	7	6	5	4	3	2	1	20	19	18	17	16	15	14	13	12	11	10
17	17	16	15	14	13	12	11	10	9	8	7	6	5	4	3	2	1	20	19	18	17	16	15	14	13	12	11
18	18	17	16	15	14	13	12	11	10	9	8	7	6	5	4	3	2	1	20	19	18	17	16	15	14	13	12
19	19	18	17	16	15	14	13	12	11	10	9	8	7	6	5	4	3	2	1	20	19	18	17	16	15	14	13
20	20	19	18	17	16	15	14	13	12	11	10	9	8	7	6	5	4	3	2	1	20	19	18	17	16	15	14
1	1	20	19	18	17	16	15	14	13	12	11	10	9	8	7	6	5	4	3	2	1	20	19	18	17	16	15
2	2	1	20	19	18	17	16	15	14	13	12	11	10	9	8	7	6	5	4	3	2	1	20	19	18	17	16
3	3	2	1	20	19	18	17	16	15	14	13	12	11	10	9	8	7	6	5	4	3	2	1	20	19	18	17
4	4	3	2	1	20	19	18	17	16	15	14	13	12	11	10	9	8	7	6	5	4	3	2	1	20	19	18
5	5	4	3	2	1	20	19	18	17	16	15	14	13	12	11	10	9	8	7	6	5	4	3	2	1	20	19
6	6	5	4	3	2	1	20	19	18	17	16	15	14	13	12	11	10	9	8	7	6	5	4	3	2	1	20
7	7	6	5	4	3	2	1	20	19	18	17	16	15	14	13	12	11	10	9	8	7	6	5	4	3	2	1
8	8	7	6	5	4	3	2	1	20	19	18	17	16	15	14	13	12	11	10	9	8	7	6	5	4	3	2
9	9	8	7	6	5	4	3	2	1	20	19	18	17	16	15	14	13	12	11	10	9	8	7	6	5	4	3
10	10	9	8	7	6	5	4	3	2	1	20	19	18	17	16	15	14	13	12	11	10	9	8	7	6	5	4
11	11	10	9	8	7	6	5	4	3	2	1	20	19	18	17	16	15	14	13	12	11	10	9	8	7	6	5
12	12	11	10	9	8	7	6	5	4	3	2	1	20	19	18	17	16	15	14	13	12	11	10	9	8	7	6
13	13	12	11	10	9	8	7	6	5	4	3	2	1	20	19	18	17	16	15	14	13	12	11	10	9	8	7
14	14	13	12	11	10	9	8	7	6	5	4	3	2	1	20	19	18	17	16	15	14	13	12	11	10	9	8
15	15	14	13	12	11	10	9	8	7	6	5	4	3	2	1	20	19	18	17	16	15	14	13	12	11	10	9
16	16	15	14	13	12	11	10	9	8	7	6	5	4	3	2	1	20	19	18	17	16	15	14	13	12	11	10
17	17	16	15	14	13	12	11	10	9	8	7	6	5	4	3	2	1	20	19	18	17	16	15	14	13	12	11
18	18	17	16	15	14	13	12	11	10	9	8	7	6	5	4	3	2	1	20	19	18	17	16	15	14	13	12
19	19	18	17	16	15	14	13	12	11	10	9	8	7	6	5	4	3	2	1	20	19	18	17	16	15	14	13
20	20	19	18	17	16	15	14	13	12	11	10	9	8	7	6	5	4	3	2	1	20	19	18	17	16	15	14

Glacier Bay

"Glacier Bay" was made as soon as I returned home from a cruise to Alaska. Compared to pictures I had seen, the glaciers I saw on the cruise were shrinking and covered in pollution. Not such a pretty sight. I felt compelled to make a quilt in memory of what the glaciers used to be.

Choosing Fabric

This quilt uses 20 fabrics in two color groups: 12 in lighter or brighter colors and 8 in a slightly darker complementary color group. Fabrics in each group should range from light to dark. For the border, I suggest a darker fabric and a bright border-accent fabric to enhance the overall appearance of your project and frame it nicely.

Materials

Yardage is based on 42"-wide fabric.

¼ yard *each* of 12 lighter/brighter bargello fabrics
¼ yard *each* of 8 slightly darker bargello fabrics
1⅜ yards of dark fabric for borders and binding
¼ yard of bright fabric for border accent
3 yards of fabric for backing
52" x 54" piece of batting

Cutting

From *each* of the 12 lighter/brighter bargello fabrics, cut:
4 strips, 1½" x 42"

From *each* of the 8 slightly darker bargello fabrics, cut:
3 strips, 1½" x 42"

From the dark fabric for borders and binding, cut:
6 strips, 3¾" x 42"
6 strips, 2¼" x 42"
5 strips, 1½" x 42"

From the bright fabric for border accent, cut:
5 strips, 1" x 42"

Fabric Map

Referring to page 8, use a scrap of each bargello fabric to create a fabric map. You'll need to refer to your map throughout the project in order to position all of the strips correctly to make the design shown.

Making the Strip Sets

1. Referring to "Building Strip Sets" on page 9 and using the 1½"-wide strips for fabrics 1–12, sew the strips together in numerical order according to your fabric map to make four identical strip sets. Press all seam allowances toward the even-numbered fabrics.
2. Using the 1½"-wide strips for fabrics 13–20, sew the strips together in numerical order according

Pieced by author and quilted by Nadia Wilson of Port Hardy, British Columbia, Canada

FINISHED SIZE: 47" x 49"

Glacier Bay

to your fabric map to make three identical strip sets. Press all seam allowances toward the even-numbered fabrics.

Fabric 1
Fabric 2
Fabric 3
Fabric 4
Fabric 5
Fabric 6
Fabric 7
Fabric 8
Fabric 9
Fabric 10
Fabric 11
Fabric 12

Make 4 strip sets.

Fabric 13
Fabric 14
Fabric 15
Fabric 16
Fabric 17
Fabric 18
Fabric 19
Fabric 20

Make 3 strip sets.

3. Join a lighter strip set from step 1 to a darker strip set from step 2 along their long edges, matching fabric 12 on the first strip set to fabric 13 on the second strip set to make a full strip set. Press the seam allowances toward fabric 12. Repeat to make a second full strip set (fabrics 1–20). You'll have three partial strip sets left over, two with fabrics 1–12 and one with fabrics 13–20. The strip sets are not used in even amounts, so making use of partial strip sets helps eliminate waste.

CREATING THE DESIGN

"Glacier Bay" is not a basic bargello design. This quilt must be built by carefully following the design chart, starting on the far left with row 1 and working to row 31 on the far right. For some of the rows, you'll be rearranging the segments so the fabrics are *not* in numerical order.

Row 1

1. From a full strip set (fabrics 1–20), cut two 2¼"-wide slices. Refer to "Cutting Slices" on page 11 as needed for guidance.
2. Referring to your fabric map, join fabric 20 on the first slice to fabric 1 on the second slice, right sides together, and using a scant ¼"-wide seam allowance. Press the seam allowances toward

fabric 20. You now have a complete row. Using your fabric map as a guide, compare your finished row to row 1 on the "Glacier Bay Design Chart" on page 42. The numbers assigned to your fabrics should be in the same order as the chart numbers for row 1. You should have 40 fabrics in your row.

Row 2

1. From a full strip set (fabrics 1–20), cut two 2"-wide slices. From a partial strip set with fabrics 13–20, cut one 2"-wide slice.
2. Referring to your fabric map and using the one full slice, remove the stitching between fabrics 1 and 2 to make a segment with fabrics 2–20.
3. Using a full slice, stitch fabric 1 to fabric 20 at the bottom of the partial row from step 2. Press the seam allowances toward fabric 20.
4. Using the partial slice, remove the stitching between fabrics 18 and 19 and between fabrics 19 and 20 to make a single piece of fabric 19. Set aside any leftover segments for possible use later.
5. Stitch fabric 19 to the bottom of the partial row from step 3. Press the seam allowances toward fabric 20. You now have a complete row. Using your fabric map as a guide, compare your finished row to row 2 on the chart. The numbers assigned to your fabrics should be in the same order as the chart numbers for row 2.

Joining the Rows

With right sides together and raw edges aligned, place row 2 on top of row 1. Using a scant ¼"-wide seam allowance and carefully matching the seam intersections with your finger, join the rows along their long edges. You may want to use a stylus or awl to hold the matched seam intersections in place, gently easing the fabric as needed to align the seams. Press the seam allowances toward the newly added row, in this case row 2.

Working from the Chart

1. Continue working in the same manner, cutting full slices and partial slices as required in the width

indicated on the chart. For rows 16 and 17 and rows 23–31, you may be able to use some of the leftover segments to complete the rows. Referring to your fabric map and using the bold lines on the chart as a guide, remove the stitching between segments as needed and join the segments in the order indicated for the row you're making. Make one row at a time, working across the chart.

2. You can join the rows as you make each new row, or you can pin rows to your design wall, and then sew the rows together after several rows are completed, whichever method works best for you. Once you've completed 10 rows, you may want to begin a new section with rows 11–21; and then build an additional section with rows 22–31. I find dividing the project into three sections makes it easier to handle.

3. Join the three sections in the correct numerical order to complete the center of the quilt top.

Borders and Finishing

For more details on any of the following steps, go to ShopMartingale.com/HowtoQuilt for free downloadable information.

1. Refer to "Multiple-Border Units" to make a border unit using the 1½"-wide inner-border strips, 1"-wide border accent strips, and the 3¾"-wide outer-border strips. Measure, cut, and sew the border unit to the quilt top. Miter the corners.

2. Layer the quilt top with batting and backing. Baste and quilt as desired. (Or take the neatly folded quilt top and backing to your professional long-arm machine quilter.)

3. Using the 2¼"-wide binding strips, make and attach the binding.

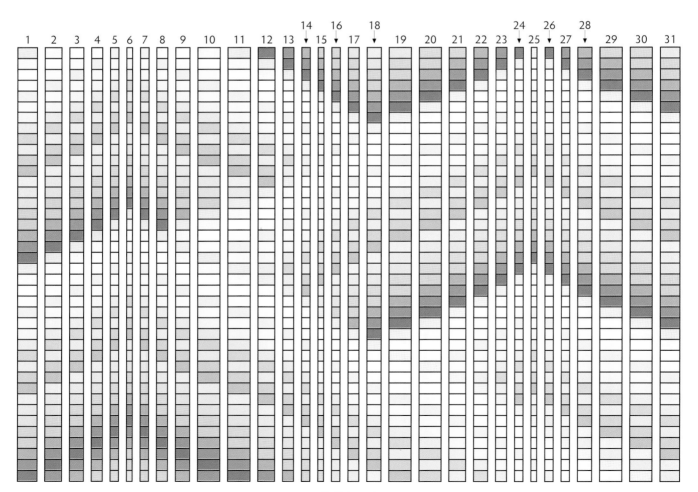

Quilt layout

MULTIPLE-BORDER UNITS

I like to add a narrow border accent in the seam between the inner and outer borders. The border strip lies toward the outer border, making that border look narrower.

1. Join the border strips at right angles, with right sides together, and stitch across the top strip diagonally as shown. Trim the excess fabric, leaving a ¼"-wide seam allowance and press the seam allowances open.

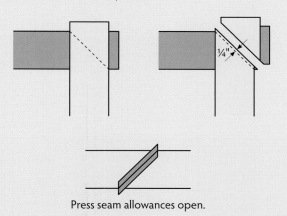

Press seam allowances open.

2. Fold the 1"-wide accent border strip in half lengthwise, wrong sides together, and press.

Fold line

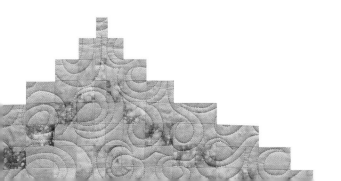

3. Align the raw edges of the accent strip with one raw edge of the outer-border strip, and machine baste in place with a ⅛"-wide seam allowance.

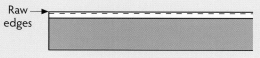

Raw edges →

Machine baste.

4. Lay the inner-border strip on top of the accent strip, right sides together and raw edges aligned. Reset the stitch length, if needed, and sew the inner-border strip to the accent strip with a very straight ¼"-wide seam allowance. Press the seam allowances toward the inner-border strip.

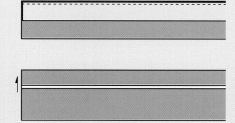

GLACIER BAY DESIGN CHART

Row number	1	2	3	4	5	6	7	8	9	10	11	12	13	14	15	16	17	18	19	20	21	22	23	24	25	26	27	28	29	30	31
Cut width of rows	2¼"	2"	1¾"	1½"	1¼"	1"	1¼"	1½"	1¾"	2½"	2½"	2"	1½"	1¼"	1"	1¼"	1½"	1¾"	2½"	2½"	2"	1¾"	1½"	1¼"	1"	1¼"	1¼"	1¾"	2½"	2½"	2¾"
Fabric number	1	2	3	4	5	6	5	4	3	2	1	20	19	18	17	16	15	14	15	16	17	18	19	20	1	20	19	18	17	16	15
	2	3	4	5	6	7	6	5	4	3	2	1	20	19	18	17	16	15	16	17	18	19	20	1	2	1	20	19	18	17	16
	3	4	5	6	7	8	7	6	5	4	3	2	1	20	19	18	17	16	17	18	19	20	1	2	3	2	1	20	19	18	17
	4	5	6	7	8	9	8	7	6	5	4	3	2	1	20	19	18	17	18	19	20	1	2	3	4	3	2	1	20	19	18
	5	6	7	8	9	10	9	8	7	6	5	4	3	2	1	20	19	18	19	20	1	2	3	4	5	4	3	2	1	20	19
	6	7	8	9	10	11	10	9	8	7	6	5	4	3	2	1	20	19	20	1	2	3	4	5	6	5	4	3	2	1	20
	7	8	9	10	11	12	11	10	9	8	7	6	5	4	3	2	1	20	1	2	3	4	5	6	7	6	5	4	3	2	1
	8	9	10	11	12	13	12	11	10	9	8	7	6	5	4	3	2	1	2	3	4	5	6	7	8	7	6	5	4	3	2
	9	10	11	12	13	14	13	12	11	10	9	8	7	6	5	4	1	2	3	4	5	6	7	8	9	8	7	6	5	4	3
	10	11	12	13	14	15	14	13	12	11	10	9	8	7	6	1	2	3	4	5	6	7	8	9	10	9	8	7	6	5	4
	11	12	13	14	15	16	15	14	13	12	11	10	9	8	1	2	3	4	5	6	7	8	9	10	11	10	9	8	7	6	5
	12	13	14	15	16	17	16	15	14	13	12	11	10	1	2	3	4	5	6	7	8	9	10	11	12	11	10	9	8	7	6
	13	14	15	16	17	18	17	16	15	14	13	12	1	2	3	4	5	6	7	8	9	10	11	12	13	12	11	10	9	8	7
	14	15	16	17	18	19	18	17	16	15	14	1	2	3	4	5	6	7	8	9	10	11	12	13	14	13	12	11	10	9	8
	15	16	17	18	19	20	19	18	17	16	1	2	3	4	5	6	7	8	9	10	11	12	13	14	15	14	13	12	11	10	9
	16	17	18	19	20	1	20	19	18	1	2	3	4	5	6	7	8	9	10	11	12	13	14	15	16	15	14	13	12	11	10
	17	18	19	20	1	2	1	20	1	2	3	4	5	6	7	8	9	10	11	12	13	14	15	16	17	16	15	14	13	12	11
	18	19	20	1	2	3	2	1	2	3	4	5	6	7	8	9	10	11	12	13	14	15	16	17	18	17	16	15	14	13	12
	19	20	1	2	3	4	3	2	1	4	5	6	7	8	9	10	11	12	13	14	15	16	17	18	19	18	17	16	15	14	13
	20	1	2	3	4	5	4	3	2	1	6	7	8	9	10	11	12	13	14	15	16	17	18	19	20	19	18	17	16	15	14
	1	2	3	4	5	6	5	4	3	2	1	8	9	10	11	12	13	14	15	16	17	18	19	20	1	20	19	18	17	16	15
	2	3	4	5	6	7	6	5	4	3	2	1	10	11	12	13	14	15	16	17	18	19	20	1	2	1	20	19	18	17	16
	3	4	5	6	7	8	7	6	5	4	3	2	1	12	13	14	15	16	17	18	19	20	1	2	3	2	1	20	19	18	17
	4	5	6	7	8	9	8	7	6	5	4	3	2	1	14	15	16	17	18	19	20	1	2	3	4	3	2	1	20	19	18
	5	6	7	8	9	10	9	8	7	6	5	4	3	2	1	16	17	18	19	20	1	2	3	4	5	4	3	2	1	20	19
	6	7	8	9	10	11	10	9	8	7	6	5	4	3	2	1	18	19	20	1	2	3	4	5	6	5	4	3	2	1	20
	7	8	9	10	11	12	11	10	9	8	7	6	5	4	3	2	1	20	1	2	3	4	5	6	7	6	5	4	3	2	1
	8	9	10	11	12	13	12	11	10	9	8	7	6	5	4	3	2	1	2	3	4	5	6	7	8	7	6	5	4	3	2
	9	10	11	12	13	14	13	12	11	10	9	8	7	6	5	4	3	2	1	4	5	6	7	8	9	8	7	6	5	4	3
	10	11	12	13	14	15	14	13	12	11	10	9	8	7	6	5	4	3	2	1	6	7	8	9	10	9	8	7	6	5	4
	11	12	13	14	15	16	15	14	13	12	11	10	9	8	7	6	5	4	3	2	1	8	9	10	11	10	9	8	7	6	5
	12	13	14	15	16	17	16	15	14	13	12	11	10	9	8	7	6	5	4	3	2	1	10	11	12	11	10	9	8	7	6
	13	14	15	16	17	18	17	16	15	14	13	12	11	10	9	8	7	6	5	4	3	2	1	12	13	12	11	10	9	8	7
	14	15	16	17	18	19	18	17	16	15	14	13	12	11	10	9	8	7	6	5	4	3	2	1	14	13	12	11	10	9	8
	15	16	17	18	19	20	19	18	17	16	15	14	13	12	11	10	9	8	7	6	5	4	3	2	1	14	13	12	11	10	9
	16	17	18	19	20	1	20	19	18	17	16	15	14	13	12	11	10	9	8	7	6	5	4	3	2	1	14	13	12	11	10
	17	18	19	20	1	2	1	20	19	18	17	16	15	14	13	12	11	10	9	8	7	6	5	4	3	2	1	14	13	12	11
	18	19	20	1	2	3	2	1	20	19	18	17	16	15	14	13	12	11	10	9	8	7	6	5	4	3	2	1	14	13	12
	19	20	19	18	17	16	17	18	19	20	19	18	17	16	15	14	13	12	11	10	9	8	7	6	5	4	3	2	1	14	13
	20	19	18	17	16	15	16	17	18	19	20	19	18	17	16	15	14	13	12	11	10	9	8	7	6	5	4	3	2	1	14

Argyle

"Argyle" is a masculine quilt, reminiscent of the sweaters I used to knit my fellas, made in green for all those readers who asked for a green quilt. This one has my friend Brenda's name on it.

Choosing Fabric

Select 20 fabrics in one color group; the colors should range in value from light to dark. Think about adding one or two zinger fabrics to the mix.

Materials

Yardage is based on 42"-wide fabric.

⅞ yard *each* of 20 bargello fabrics
⅞ yard of dark fabric for binding
3¼ yards of 108"-wide quilt backing*
100" x 101" piece of batting

*If using 42"-wide fabric, you'll need 9 yards.

Cutting

From *each* of the 20 bargello fabrics, cut:
10 strips, 2½" x 42"

From the dark binding fabric, cut:
10 strips, 2¼" x 42"

Fabric Map

Referring to page 8, use a scrap of each bargello fabric to create a fabric map. You'll need to refer to your map throughout the project in order to position all of the strips correctly to make the design shown.

Making the Strip Sets

Referring to "Building Strip Sets" on page 9 and using the 2½"-wide bargello fabric strips, sew the strips together in numerical order according to your fabric map to make nine identical strip sets. Press all seam allowances toward the even-numbered fabrics. Wait to make the tenth strip set until you see how many leftover segments you can utilize. You might find that nine strip sets will be sufficient.

Fabric 1
Fabric 2
Fabric 3
Fabric 4
Fabric 5
Fabric 6
Fabric 7
Fabric 8
Fabric 9
Fabric 10
Fabric 11
Fabric 12
Fabric 13
Fabric 14
Fabric 15
Fabric 16
Fabric 17
Fabric 18
Fabric 19
Fabric 20

Make 9 strip sets.

Pieced by author and machine quilted by Jennifer Mummery of East Sooke, British Columbia, Canada

FINISHED SIZE: 96" x 94½"

SYMMETRICAL QUILT

"Argyle" is a symmetrical quilt, so you'll need to make an identical pair of each row, except for row 35, which is the center row of the quilt. If you have a large design wall, make a few rows and pin them to your design wall, positioning one section on the left and the mirror-image section on the right.

Row 1

Make two identical rows.

1. Cut eight 2"-wide slices. Refer to "Cutting Slices" on page 11 as needed for guidance.
2. Referring to your fabric map and using one slice, remove the stitching between fabrics 10 and 11 to make a segment with fabrics 1–10. On the same slice, remove the stitching between fabrics 12 and 13 to make a segment with fabrics 13–20. Sew fabric 1 to fabric 20 to make a section with 18 fabrics. Fabric 13 becomes the bottom of the row.
3. On a full slice, remove the stitching between fabrics 15 and 16 to make a segment with fabrics 16–20. Stitch fabric 20 to fabric 13 on the bottom of the partial row from step 2. Fabric 16 will now be the bottom of the row.
4. On another slice, remove the stitching between fabrics 14 and 15 to make a segment with fabrics 15–20. Stitch fabric 15 to fabric 16 on the bottom of the partial row from step 3. Fabric 20 will now be the bottom of the row.
5. On a full slice, remove the stitching between fabrics 12 and 13 to make a segment with fabrics 13–20. On the same slice, remove the stitching between fabrics 10 and 11 to make a segment with fabrics 1–10. Sew fabric 1 to fabric 20 to make a section with 18 fabrics. Then sew fabric 13 to the bottom of the partial row from step 4. You now have a complete row. In the same manner, make a second identical row 1. Press all seam allowances toward the even-numbered

fabrics. Set aside any leftover segments for possible use later.
6. Compare the two rows to each other and to the "Argyle Design Chart" on page 48. The numbers assigned to your fabrics should be in the same order as the chart numbers for row 1. You should have 47 fabrics in your row.

Row 2

Make two identical rows.

1. Cut eight 2¼"-wide slices.
2. Referring to your fabric map and using one slice, remove the stitching between fabrics 11 and 12 to make a segment with fabrics 1–11. On the same slice, remove the stitching between fabrics 14 and 15 to make a segment with fabrics 15–20. Sew fabric 1 to fabric 20 to make a section with 17 fabrics. Fabric 15 becomes the bottom of the row.
3. On a full slice, remove the stitching between fabrics 14 and 15 to make a segment with fabrics 15–20. Stitch fabric 20 to fabric 15 on the bottom of the partial row from step 2. Fabric 15 will now be the bottom of the row.
4. On another slice, remove the stitching between fabrics 13 and 14 to make a segment with fabrics 14–20. Stitch fabric 14 to fabric 15 on the bottom of the partial row from step 3. Fabric 20 will now be the bottom of the row.
5. On a full slice, remove the stitching between fabrics 14 and 15 to make a segment with fabrics 15–20. On the same slice, remove the stitching between fabrics 11 and 12 to make a segment with fabrics 1–11. Sew fabric 1 to fabric 20 to make a section with 17 fabrics. Then sew fabric 15 to the bottom of the partial row from step 4. You now have a complete row. In the same manner, make a second identical row 2. Press all seam allowances toward the even-numbered fabrics. Set aside any leftover segments for possible use later.
6. Compare the two rows to each other and to the chart for accuracy. They should be the same length and in the number sequence indicated on the chart.

ORGANIZE LEFTOVER SEGMENTS

You may find it helpful to organize your leftover segments by pinning them to your design wall, grouping segments from slices of equal width together. Starting with row 7, you may be able to use some of the segments to build part of the rows.

Joining the Rows

1. With right sides together and raw edges aligned, place row 2 on top of row 1. Using a scant ¼"-wide seam allowance and carefully matching the seam intersections with your finger, join the rows along their long edges. You may want to use a stylus or awl to hold the matched seam intersections in place, gently easing the fabric as needed to align the seams. Press the seam allowances toward the newly added row, in this case row 2.

2. In the same manner, sew the second row 2 on top of the second row 1 and press the seam allowances as before.

Working from the Chart

1. Continue working in this manner; for each pair of rows, cut eight slices in the width indicated on the chart for rows 3–6, rows 10–12, and row 23. Cut four to eight slices in the width indicated on the chart for the remaining rows. The number of slices you'll need will depend on the row you're building and how many leftover segments you can utilize. Referring to your fabric map and using the bold lines on the chart as a guide, remove the stitching between segments, as needed, and join the segments in the order indicated for the row you're making. Each time you'll be making two identical rows, except for row 35.

2. You can join the rows as you make each new row, pressing the seam allowances toward the newly added rows. Or, you can pin rows to your design wall, and then sew the rows together after several rows are completed, whichever method works best for you.

3. Once you've completed 11 rows, you may want to begin a new section with rows 12–22, and then build an additional section with rows 23–34. I find dividing the project into sections makes it easier to handle. Make sure you have a left side and mirror-image right side that can be joined with row 35.

4. Join the sections in the correct numerical order to complete the symmetrical design for the left half of the quilt. Repeat to make the right half of the quilt, sewing these rows from the bottom to the top.

Row 35

Row 35 is the middle of your quilt.

1. Cut two 1"-wide slices.

2. Referring to your fabric map and using one slice, remove the stitching between fabrics 1 and 2 to make a segment with fabrics 2–20.

3. Use a full slice (fabrics 1–20) and stitch fabric 1 to fabric 2 on the segment from step 2. You should have fabric 20 at the top and bottom of your row.

4. Use a leftover segment with fabrics 1–4 and stitch fabric 1 to fabric 20. Repeat to sew a second leftover segment (fabrics 1–4) to fabric 20 on the opposite end of the row. You now have a complete row. The numbers assigned to your fabrics should be in the same order as the chart numbers for row 35. You should have 47 fabrics in your row.

SEAM-ALLOWANCES CHECK

Remember to check the back of the quilt for errant seam allowances that aren't lying flat, and press them in the proper direction. A flat, neat back will ensure a smoother and nicer-looking quilt.

Assembly

1. Referring to the chart and using a scant ¼"-wide seam allowance, join the left and right halves of the quilt to row 35 to complete the quilt top. Press the seam allowances toward the center.

2. Finish by basting around the quilt top about ⅛" from the outer edges to stabilize the seams for quilting.

MAKE IT KING SIZE

If you want a larger quilt, simply add a 5"- or 6"-wide border, and your quilt will be 10" or 12" larger. See "Gallery of Quilts" on page 76.

Finishing

For more details on the following steps, go to ShopMartingale.com/HowtoQuilt for free downloadable information.

1. Layer the quilt top with batting and backing. Baste and quilt as desired. (Or take the neatly folded quilt top and backing to your professional long-arm machine quilter.)

2. Using the 2¼"-wide binding strips, make and attach the binding.

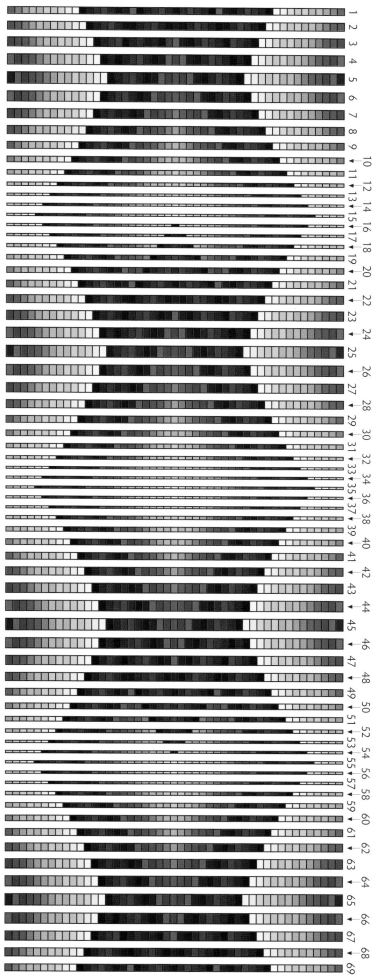

Quilt layout

ARGYLE DESIGN CHART

Row number	1	2	3	4	5	6	7	8	9	10	11	12	13	14	15	16	17	18	19	20
Cut width of rows	2"	2¼"	2½"	2¾"	3"	2¾"	2½"	2¼"	2"	1¾"	1½"	1¼"	1"	1"	1"	1"	1"	1¼"	1½"	1¾"
Fabric number	10	11	12	13	14	13	12	11	10	9	8	7	6	5	4	5	6	7	8	9
	9	10	11	12	13	12	11	10	9	8	7	6	5	4	3	4	5	6	7	8
	8	9	10	11	12	11	10	9	8	7	6	5	4	3	2	3	4	5	6	7
	7	8	9	10	11	10	9	8	7	6	5	4	3	2	1	2	3	4	5	6
	6	7	8	9	10	9	8	7	6	5	4	3	2	1	20	1	2	3	4	5
	5	6	7	8	9	8	7	6	5	4	3	2	1	20	19	20	1	2	3	4
	4	5	6	7	8	7	6	5	4	3	2	1	20	19	18	19	20	1	2	3
	3	4	5	6	7	6	5	4	3	2	1	20	19	18	17	18	19	20	1	2
	2	3	4	5	6	5	4	3	2	1	20	19	18	17	16	17	18	19	20	1
	1	2	3	4	5	4	3	2	1	20	19	18	17	16	15	16	17	18	19	20
	20	1	2	3	4	3	2	1	20	19	18	17	16	15	14	15	16	17	18	19
	19	20	1	2	3	2	1	20	19	18	17	16	15	14	13	14	15	16	17	18
	18	19	20	1	2	1	20	19	18	17	16	15	14	13	12	13	14	15	16	17
	17	18	19	20	1	20	19	18	17	16	15	14	13	12	11	12	13	14	15	16
	16	17	18	19	20	19	18	17	16	15	14	13	12	11	10	11	12	13	14	15
	15	16	17	20	19	18	17	16	15	14	13	12	11	10	9	10	11	12	13	14
	14	15	20	19	18	17	16	15	14	13	12	11	10	9	8	9	10	11	12	13
	13	20	19	18	17	16	15	14	13	12	11	10	9	8	7	8	9	10	11	12
	20	19	18	17	16	15	14	13	12	11	10	9	8	7	6	7	8	9	10	11
	19	18	17	16	15	14	13	12	11	10	9	8	7	6	5	6	7	8	9	20
	18	17	16	15	14	13	12	11	10	9	8	7	6	5	4	5	6	7	20	19
	17	16	15	14	13	12	11	10	9	8	7	6	5	4	3	4	5	20	19	18
	16	15	14	13	12	11	10	9	8	7	6	5	4	3	2	3	20	19	18	17
	15	14	13	12	11	10	9	8	7	6	5	4	3	2	1	20	19	18	17	16
	16	15	14	13	12	11	10	9	8	7	6	5	4	3	2	3	20	19	18	17
	17	16	15	14	13	12	11	10	9	8	7	6	5	4	3	4	5	20	19	18
	18	17	16	15	14	13	12	11	10	9	8	7	6	5	4	5	6	7	20	19
	19	18	17	16	15	14	13	12	11	10	9	8	7	6	5	6	7	8	9	20
	20	19	18	17	16	15	14	13	12	11	10	9	8	7	6	7	8	9	10	11
	13	20	19	18	17	16	15	14	13	12	11	10	9	8	7	8	9	10	11	12
	14	15	20	19	18	17	16	15	14	13	12	11	10	9	8	9	10	11	12	13
	15	16	17	20	19	18	17	16	15	14	13	12	11	10	9	10	11	12	13	14
	16	17	18	19	20	19	18	17	16	15	14	13	12	11	10	11	12	13	14	15
	17	18	19	20	1	20	19	18	17	16	15	14	13	12	11	12	13	14	15	16
	18	19	20	1	2	1	20	19	18	17	16	15	14	13	12	13	14	15	16	17
	19	20	1	2	3	2	1	20	19	18	17	16	15	14	13	14	15	16	17	18
	20	1	2	3	4	3	2	1	20	19	18	17	16	15	14	15	16	17	18	19
	1	2	3	4	5	4	3	2	1	20	19	18	17	16	15	16	17	18	19	20
	2	3	4	5	6	5	4	3	2	1	20	19	18	17	16	17	18	19	20	1
	3	4	5	6	7	6	5	4	3	2	1	20	19	18	17	18	19	20	1	2
	4	5	6	7	8	7	6	5	4	3	2	1	20	19	18	19	20	1	2	3
	5	6	7	8	9	8	7	6	5	4	3	2	1	20	19	20	1	2	3	4
	6	7	8	9	10	9	8	7	6	5	4	3	2	1	20	1	2	3	4	5
	7	8	9	10	11	10	9	8	7	6	5	4	3	2	1	2	3	4	5	6
	8	9	10	11	12	11	10	9	8	7	6	5	4	3	2	3	4	5	6	7
	9	10	11	12	13	12	11	10	9	8	7	6	5	4	3	4	5	6	7	8
	10	11	12	13	14	13	12	11	10	9	8	7	6	5	4	5	6	7	8	9

Row number	21	22	23	24	25	26	27	28	29	30	31	32	33	34	35
Cut width of rows	2"	2¼"	2½"	2¾"	3"	2¾"	2½"	2¼"	2"	1¾"	1½"	1¼"	1"	1"	1"
Fabric number	10	11	12	13	14	13	12	11	10	9	8	7	6	5	4
	9	10	11	12	13	12	11	10	9	8	7	6	5	4	3
	8	9	10	11	12	11	10	9	8	7	6	5	4	3	2
	7	8	9	10	11	10	9	8	7	6	5	4	3	2	1
	6	7	8	9	10	9	8	7	6	5	4	3	2	1	20
	5	6	7	8	9	8	7	6	5	4	3	2	1	20	19
	4	5	6	7	8	7	6	5	4	3	2	1	20	19	18
	3	4	5	6	7	6	5	4	3	2	1	20	19	18	17
	2	3	4	5	6	5	4	3	2	1	20	19	18	17	16
	1	2	3	4	5	4	3	2	1	20	19	18	17	16	15
	20	1	2	3	4	3	2	1	20	19	18	17	16	15	14
	19	20	1	2	3	2	1	20	19	18	17	16	15	14	13
	18	19	20	1	2	1	20	19	18	17	16	15	14	13	12
	17	18	19	20	1	20	19	18	17	16	15	14	13	12	11
	16	17	18	19	20	19	18	17	16	15	14	13	12	11	10
	15	16	17	20	19	18	17	16	15	14	13	12	11	10	9
	14	15	20	19	18	17	16	15	14	13	12	11	10	9	8
	13	20	19	18	17	16	15	14	13	12	11	10	9	8	7
	20	19	18	17	16	15	14	13	12	11	10	9	8	7	6
	19	18	17	16	15	14	13	12	11	10	9	8	7	6	5
	18	17	16	15	14	13	12	11	10	9	8	7	6	5	4
	17	16	15	14	13	12	11	10	9	8	7	6	5	4	3
	16	15	14	13	12	11	10	9	8	7	6	5	4	3	2
	15	14	13	12	11	10	9	8	7	6	5	4	3	2	1
	16	15	14	13	12	11	10	9	8	7	6	5	4	3	2
	17	16	15	14	13	12	11	10	9	8	7	6	5	4	3
	18	17	16	15	14	13	12	11	10	9	8	7	6	5	4
	19	18	17	16	15	14	13	12	11	10	9	8	7	6	5
	20	19	18	17	16	15	14	13	12	11	10	9	8	7	6
	13	20	19	18	17	16	15	14	13	12	11	10	9	8	7
	14	15	20	19	18	17	16	15	14	13	12	11	10	9	8
	15	16	17	20	19	18	17	16	15	14	13	12	11	10	9
	16	17	18	19	20	19	18	17	16	15	14	13	12	11	10
	17	18	19	20	1	20	19	18	17	16	15	14	13	12	11
	18	19	20	1	2	1	20	19	18	17	16	15	14	13	12
	19	20	1	2	3	2	1	20	19	18	17	16	15	14	13
	20	1	2	3	4	3	2	1	20	19	18	17	16	15	14
	1	2	3	4	5	4	3	2	1	20	19	18	17	16	15
	2	3	4	5	6	5	4	3	2	1	20	19	18	17	16
	3	4	5	6	7	6	5	4	3	2	1	20	19	18	17
	4	5	6	7	8	7	6	5	4	3	2	1	20	19	18
	5	6	7	8	9	8	7	6	5	4	3	2	1	20	19
	6	7	8	9	10	9	8	7	6	5	4	3	2	1	20
	7	8	9	10	11	10	9	8	7	6	5	4	3	2	1
	8	9	10	11	12	11	10	9	8	7	6	5	4	3	2
	9	10	11	12	13	12	11	10	9	8	7	6	5	4	3
	10	11	12	13	14	13	12	11	10	9	8	7	6	5	4

Pieced by author and machine quilted by Jennifer Mummery of East Sooke, British Columbia, Canada

FINISHED SIZE: 45½" x 64½"

Marmalade

"Marmalade" was another idea that floated around in my head for a long time. Once I had collected the necessary 30 fabrics, the rest was easy. Many quilters asked for a more traditional version of "Qualicum Zephyr" in my book Twist-and-Turn Bargello Quilts *(Martingale, 2009). And I must admit, this was always the vision in my head.*

Choosing Fabric

This quilt uses 30 fabrics in three color groups (lime, orange, and yellow), plus a background fabric. In each group, you'll need 10 fabrics in one color: 5 light fabrics for the front of the ribbon and 5 darker fabrics for the back of the ribbon. Fabrics in each color group should range from light to dark.

I used a dark-green fabric for my background, but you may want to try a different color, depending on your ribbon-color choice. I prefer a background fabric that has visual texture. These fabrics add life and dimension to the project, so the ribbons appear to float on the background.

Materials

Yardage is based on 42"-wide fabric.

¼ yard *each* of 30 bargello fabrics

2¾ yards of dark fabric for ribbon background, borders, and binding

3 yards of fabric for backing

51" x 70" piece of batting

Cutting

From *each* of the 10 fabrics for the longest ribbon, cut:
3 strips, 1½" x 42" (label as fabrics 1–10)

From *each* of 5 fabrics for the middle ribbon, cut:
3 strips, 1½" x 42" (label as fabrics 1–5)

From *each* of 3 fabrics for the middle ribbon, cut:
2 strips, 1½" x 42" (label as fabrics 6–8)

From *each* of 2 fabrics for the middle ribbon, cut:
3 strips, 1½" x 42" (label as fabrics 9 and 10)

From *each* of the 10 fabrics for the shortest ribbon, cut:
2 strips, 1½" x 42" (label as fabrics 1–10)

Continued on page 52.

From the dark background fabric, cut:

24 strips, 1½" x 42"; crosscut 4 of the strips in half
    to yield 8 strips, 1½" x 21"

3 strips, 1¼" x 42"; crosscut into:
    2 strips, 1¼" x 23½"
    2 strips, 1¼" x 13½"
    3 strips, 1¼" x 5½"
    2 strips, 1¼" x 3½"
    3 strips, 1¼" x 1½"

3 strips, 1¾" x 42"; crosscut into:
    2 strips, 1¾" x 23"
    2 strips, 1¾" x 13"
    3 strips, 1¾" x 5"
    2 strips, 1¾" x 3"
    3 strips, 1¾" x 2"

7 strips, 2½" x 42"; crosscut into:
    2 strips, 2½" x 22½"
    2 strips, 2½" x 22"
    1 strip, 2½" x 21½"
    2 strips, 2½" x 12½"
    2 strips, 2½" x 12"
    1 strip, 2½" x 11½"
    3 strips, 2½" x 4½"
    3 strips, 2½" x 4"
    3 strips, 2½" x 3½"
    3 strips, 2½" x 3"
    5 squares, 2½" x 2½"
    2 strips, 2" x 2½"
    1 strip, 1½" x 2½"

4 strips, 2" x 42"

6 strips, 2¼" x 42"

SORTING THE BACKGROUND PIECES

Sort all of the dark background strips into a pile with the shortest pieces on top and the longest on the bottom, no matter the cut width. This way they'll be in the order you'll need for building the rows.

Fabric Map

Referring to page 8, use a scrap of each bargello fabric to create a fabric map showing your fabrics in light-to-dark order with their assigned numbers from 1–10 (fabric 1 is the lightest fabric, and fabric 10 is the darkest one in each color group). You'll need to refer to your map throughout the project in order to position all of the strips correctly to make the design shown.

Making the Strip Sets

1. Referring to "Building Strip Sets" on page 9 and using the 1½"-wide bargello fabrics for the longest ribbon, sew five lighter strips (fabrics 1–5) together in numerical order according to your fabric map to make three identical strip sets. Press all seam allowances toward fabric 1. Sew five darker strips (fabrics 6–10) together in numerical order according to your fabric map to make three identical strip sets. Press all seam allowances toward fabric 10.

Fabric 1		Fabric 6
Fabric 2		Fabric 7
Fabric 3		Fabric 8
Fabric 4		Fabric 9
Fabric 5		Fabric 10

Make 3 of each.

2. In the same manner, use strips 1–5 for the middle ribbon to make three strip sets. Press all seam allowances toward fabric 1. Use strips 6–10 for the middle ribbon to make two strip sets and press all seam allowances toward fabric 10. Then use strips 9 and 10 to make one additional strip set; pressing the seam allowances toward fabric 10.

3. Repeat step 1 to make a total of four strip sets, two of each, using strips 1–5 and 6–10 for the shortest ribbon.

4. Sew eight 1½"-wide background strips together to make a strip set. Press the seam allowances in one direction. (The segments from this strip set can be turned upside down when an alternate direction of seam allowance is required.) Make two full-width (42"-long) strip sets and one half-width (21"-long) strip set.

USE A DESIGN WALL

A design wall of some kind is imperative to building this project. You can use the top of your ironing board if no wall space is available. I found it easier to lay out all the pieces for the entire ribbon on my design wall before stitching the pieces together. That way I could correct any errors prior to sewing.

Longest Ribbon

You'll be working on one ribbon at a time. Each ribbon consists of nine rows. Building each ribbon, and then keeping it on your design wall while constructing the next ribbon will make the project easier.

Row 1

1. Using a fabric 1–5 strip set and a fabric 6–10 strip set for the longest ribbon, cut six 1¼"-wide slices from each strip set. Refer to "Cutting Slices" on page 11 as needed for guidance.
2. On each fabric 6–10 slice, remove the stitching between fabrics 6 and 7. Use the single piece of fabric for this row; set aside the remaining segment (fabrics 7–10) for possible use later.
3. From a background strip set, cut three 1¼"-wide slices.
4. On the background slices, remove the stitching between the fabrics 4 and 5 to make six segments with four fabrics each.
5. Using your fabric map and the bold lines on the "Marmalade Design Chart" on pages 56 and 57 as a guide, position a 1¼" x 1½" background strip on your design wall for the top of the row. Then position a fabric 1–5 slice below the background strip. Then position a four-fabric background segment, followed by a single piece of fabric 6. Continue in this manner, adding a fabric 1–5 slice, a four-fabric background segment, and a single piece of fabric 6, and so on as indicated on the chart. Lastly, position a 1¼" x 3½" background strip at the bottom to complete the row.

6. Check and make sure the numbers assigned to your fabric are in the same order as the chart for row 1. You should have 62 fabrics in your row.
7. Sew the segments together in the order indicated on the chart. Rotate the background segments as needed, so that the seam allowances on the background are going in the same direction as the ribbon-fabric segments. Check the pressing direction of the entire strip; make sure all seam allowances are pressed toward the top of the row.

Row 2

1. Using a fabric 1–5 strip set and a fabric 6–10 strip set for the longest ribbon, cut six 1¾"-wide slices from each strip set. Refer to "Cutting Slices" as needed for guidance.
2. On each fabric 6–10 slice, remove the stitching between fabrics 7 and 8. Use the two-segment pieces for this row; set aside the remaining segment (fabrics 8–10) for possible use later.
3. From a background strip set, cut three 1¾"-wide slices.
4. On the background slices, remove the stitching between the fabrics 3 and 4 *and* between 6 and 7 to make a total of six segments with three fabrics each. Set aside the remaining two-fabric segments for possible use later.
5. In the same manner as before, position the segments on your design wall. Position a 1¾" x 2" background strip at the top of the row and a 1¾" x 3" background strip at the bottom of the row. Check and make sure the numbers assigned to your fabrics are in the same order as the chart for row 2.
6. Sew the segments together in the order indicated on the chart. Rotate the background segments as needed, so that the seam allowances on the background are going in the same direction as the ribbon-fabric segments. Check the pressing direction of the entire strip; make sure all seam allowances are pressed toward the bottom of the row.
7. Lay the row on your ironing board side by side with row 1; they should be the same length.

STEPPING DOWN

Unlike the other quilts in the book (except "Möbius" on page 69), the rows in this quilt step down half of the strip width. Therefore, there are no seam intersections to use as matching points when joining the rows. The seam line of a subsequent row falls at the midpoint of each strip in the previous row.

To create midpoints for matching, fold a row in half every 6 to 8 fabrics and match the seam lines; finger-press to make a crease. When adding the next row, match the seam lines with the center crease on the adjoining row. You may also find that when the new row is wider than the previous row, you can align the seam lines on the new row with the seam lines on the previously sewn row.

Joining the Rows

With right sides together and raw edges aligned, place row 2 on top of row 1. Align the top and bottom edges and stagger the seam lines ½" as shown in the quilt layout diagram on page 55. Using a scant ¼"-wide seam allowance, join the rows along their long edges, gently easing the fabric as needed. Press the seam allowances toward the newly added row, in this case row 2.

Working from the Chart

1. Continue working in the same manner, building one row at a time. Once you've completed rows 1–9 for the longest ribbon, begin a new section with rows 10–18 for the middle ribbon. Refer to your fabric map and the chart to join the segments in the order indicated for the row you're making.

2. After completing each new row, check that it matches the chart and that the seam allowances are pressed in the correct direction.

3. Join each new row to the section you're constructing and press the seam allowances toward the newly added row.

Middle Ribbon and Shortest Ribbon

1. Use the strip sets for the middle ribbon and continue in the same manner as before.

2. Using the chart, count the number of times fabric 1 and fabric 6 are repeated in the row you're building and cut that number of slices from the appropriate strip set, in the width indicated on the chart for the row you're making.

3. From the background strip sets, cut slices in the width indicated on the chart for the row you're making. Using the bold line on the chart as a guide, remove the stitching between segments in the same manner as before. You may be able to utilize some of the leftover background segments.

4. Repeat steps 2 and 3 using the strip sets for the shortest ribbon.

Assembly

1. Join the three sections in the correct sequence to complete the quilt top. Press the seam allowances in the same direction as before.

2. Join 2"-wide background strips end to end to make a long strip. Measure the length of the quilt top. From the strip, cut two strips to this length and sew them to the sides of the quilt top. Press the seam allowances toward the borders.

3. Check the back of the quilt top, making sure all seam allowances are pressed neatly in the correct direction. Finish by basting around the quilt top about ⅛" from the outer edges to stabilize the seams for quilting.

Finishing

For more details on any of the following steps, go to ShopMartingale.com/HowtoQuilt for free download-able information.

1. Layer the quilt top with batting and backing. Baste and quilt as desired. (Or take the neatly folded quilt top and backing to your professional long-arm machine quilter.)
2. Using the 2¼"-wide binding strips, make and attach the binding.

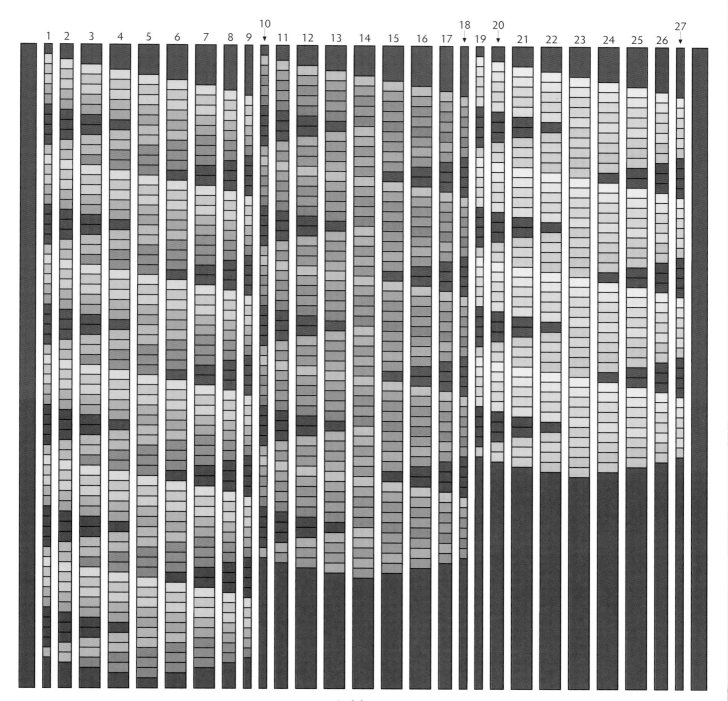

Quilt layout

MARMALADE DESIGN CHART

The letter B on the chart refers to a strip of background fabric. Use a single strip in the length indicated at the top and bottom of each row.

Row number	1	2	3	4	5	6	7	8	9	10	11	12	13	14	15	16	17	18	19	20	21	22	23	24	25	26	27
Cut width of row	1¼"	1¾"	2½"	2½"	2½"	2½"	2½"	1¾"	1¼"	1¼"	1¾"	2½"	2½"	2½"	2½"	2½"	1¾"	1¼"	1¼"	1¾"	2½"	2½"	2½"	2½"	2½"	1¾"	1¼"
Fabric number	B1½"	B2"	B2½"	B3"	B3½"	B4"	B4½"	B5"	B5½"	B1½"	B2"	B2½"	B3"	B3½"	B4"	B4½"	B5"	B5½"	B1½"	B2"	B2½"	B3"	B3½"	B4"	B4½"	B5"	B5½"
	1	1	1	1	1	1	1	1	1	1	1	1	1	1	1	1	1	1	1	1	1	1	1	1	1	1	1
	2	2	2	2	2	2	2	2	2	2	2	2	2	2	2	2	2	2	2	2	2	2	2	2	2	2	2
	3	3	3	3	3	3	3	3	3	3	3	3	3	3	3	3	3	3	3	3	3	3	3	3	3	3	3
	4	4	4	4	4	4	4	4	4	4	4	4	4	4	4	4	4	4	4	4	4	4	4	4	4	4	4
	5	5	5	5	5	5	5	5	5	5	5	5	5	5	5	5	5	5	5	5	5	5	5	5	5	5	5
	B	B	B	B	6	7	8	9	10	B	B	B	B	6	7	8	9	10	B	B	B	B	6	7	8	9	10
	B	B	B	6	7	8	9	10	B	B	B	B	6	7	8	9	10	B	B	B	B	6	7	8	9	10	B
	B	B	6	7	8	9	10	B	B	B	B	6	7	8	9	10	B	B	B	B	6	7	8	9	10	B	B
	B	6	7	8	9	10	B	B	B	B	6	7	8	9	10	B	B	B	B	6	7	8	9	10	B	B	B
	6	7	8	9	10	B	B	B	B	6	7	8	9	10	B	B	B	B	6	7	8	9	10	B	B	B	B
	1	1	1	1	1	1	1	1	1	1	1	1	1	1	1	1	1	1	1	1	1	1	1	1	1	1	1
	2	2	2	2	2	2	2	2	2	2	2	2	2	2	2	2	2	2	2	2	2	2	2	2	2	2	2
	3	3	3	3	3	3	3	3	3	3	3	3	3	3	3	3	3	3	3	3	3	3	3	3	3	3	3
	4	4	4	4	4	4	4	4	4	4	4	4	4	4	4	4	4	4	4	4	4	4	4	4	4	4	4
	5	5	5	5	5	5	5	5	5	5	5	5	5	5	5	5	5	5	5	5	5	5	5	5	5	5	5
	B	B	B	B	6	7	8	9	10	B	B	B	B	6	7	8	9	10	B	B	B	B	6	7	8	9	10
	B	B	B	6	7	8	9	10	B	B	B	B	6	7	8	9	10	B	B	B	B	6	7	8	9	10	B
	B	B	6	7	8	9	10	B	B	B	B	6	7	8	9	10	B	B	B	B	6	7	8	9	10	B	B
	B	6	7	8	9	10	B	B	B	B	6	7	8	9	10	B	B	B	B	6	7	8	9	10	B	B	B
	6	7	8	9	10	B	B	B	B	6	7	8	9	10	B	B	B	B	6	7	8	9	10	B	B	B	B

Fabric number

1	1	1	1	1	1	1	1	1	1	1	1	1	1	1	1	1	1	1	1	1	1
2	2	2	2	2	2	2	2	2	2	2	2	2	2	2	2	2	2	2	2	2	2
3	3	3	3	3	3	3	3	3	3	3	3	3	3	3	3	3	3	3	3	3	3
4	4	4	4	4	4	4	4	4	4	4	4	4	4	4	4	4	4	4	4	4	4
5	5	5	5	5	5	5	5	5	5	5	5	5	5	5	5	5	5	5	5	5	5
B	B	B	B	6	10	9	8	7	6	B	10	9	8	7	6	B	10	9	8	7	6
B	B	B	6	7	9	10	9	8	7	B	B	10	9	8	7	B	B	10	9	8	7
B	B	6	7	8	B23½	B23	B22½	9	8	B	B	B	10	9	8	B	B	B	10	9	8
B	6	7	8	9			B22	B21½	9	B	B	B	B	10	9	B	B	B	B	10	9
6	7	8	9	10					10	6	B	B	B	B	10	6	B	B	B	B	10

(design grid continues — values 1–5, B, and 6–10 with dimension labels B23½", B23", B22½", B22", B21½", B22½", 22", B13½", B13", B12½", B12", B11½", B12½", B12", B13½", B13", B3½", B3", B2½", B2", B1½", B2", B2½", B3", B3½")

Pieced by author and machine quilted by Fran Henney of Parksville, British Columbia, Canada

FINISHED SIZE: 95½" x 96½"

Island Sunrise

A bed-sized version of "Island Sunset" was the most frequent request I received following the release of Twist-and-Turn Bargello Quilts. *Based on my experience with twisted bargello quilts, I find that simply enlarging the strip widths in an existing design is not very effective. This is a complete redraft of the smaller quilt from my last book.*

Choosing Fabric

Select 20 fabrics in one color group; the colors should range in value from light to dark. I chose a color wash of batiks with each fabric blending smoothly from one to the next.

For a completely different idea, see "Rhapsody in Red" on page 79. Fran Henney used tan and red fabrics for a completely different look. Don't be afraid to use fabrics that you like. If you choose two color groups, use an uneven split of colors—9 and 11 or 8 and 12. The second color group should range from light to dark after the darkest fabric in the first group.

Materials

Yardage is based on 42"-wide fabric.

⅞ yard *each* of 20 bargello fabrics
¾ yard of dark fabric for binding
3¼ yards of 108"-wide fabric for backing*
101" x 102" piece of batting

*If using 42"-wide fabric, you'll need 9 yards.

Cutting

From *each* of the 20 bargello fabrics, cut:
9 or 10 strips, 2½" x 42"

From the dark fabric for binding, cut:
10 strips, 2¼" x 42"

Fabric Map

Referring to page 8, use a scrap of each bargello fabric to create a fabric map. You'll need to refer to your map throughout the project in order to position all of the strips correctly to make the design shown.

Making the Strip Sets

Referring to "Building Strip Sets" on page 9 and using the 2½"-wide bargello fabric strips, sew the strips together in numerical sequence according to your fabric map to make nine identical strip sets. Press all seam allowances toward the even-numbered fabric.

Fabric 1
Fabric 2
Fabric 3
Fabric 4
Fabric 5
Fabric 6
Fabric 7
Fabric 8
Fabric 9
Fabric 10
Fabric 11
Fabric 12
Fabric 13
Fabric 14
Fabric 15
Fabric 16
Fabric 17
Fabric 18
Fabric 19
Fabric 20

Make 9 strip sets.

Row 1

Row 1 is the middle of your quilt.

1. Cut three 1"-wide slices. Refer to "Cutting Slices" on page 11 as needed for guidance.
2. Referring to your fabric map and using one slice, remove the stitching between fabrics 14 and 15 to make a segment with fabrics 15–20. Set aside the leftover segment for step 5.
3. Using a full slice (fabrics 1–20) stitch fabric 1 to fabric 20 on the segment from step 2. Fabric 15 becomes the top of row 1.
4. On the remaining slice (fabrics 1–20), remove the stitching between fabrics 16 and 17 and between fabrics 6 and 7 to make a segment with fabrics 7–16. Set aside the leftover segment for step 6. Stitch fabric 16 to fabric 20 on the bottom of the partial row from step 3. Fabric 7 will now be at the bottom of the row.
5. On the leftover segment from step 2, remove the stitching between fabrics 8 and 9 to make a segment with fabrics 1–8. Stitch fabric 1 to fabric 7 on the bottom of the partial row from step 4. Fabric 8 will now be at the bottom of the row.
6. On the leftover segment from step 4, remove the stitching between fabrics 4 and 5 to make a four-fabric segment. Stitch fabric 1 to fabric 8 on the bottom of the row. You now have a complete row. Set aside any leftover segments for possible use later.
7. Using your fabric map as a guide, compare your finished row to row 1 on the "Island Sunrise Design Chart" on page 64. The numbers assigned to your fabrics should be in the same order as the chart numbers for row 1. You should have 48 fabrics in your row. Check the pressing direction of the entire strip; make sure all seam allowances are pressed toward the even-numbered fabrics.

Row 2

Make two identical rows.

1. Cut six 1¼"-wide slices.
2. Referring to your fabric map and using one slice, remove the stitching between fabrics 15 and 16 to make a segment with fabrics 16–20. Fabric 16 becomes the top of row 2. Set aside the leftover segment for step 7.
3. Use a full slice (fabrics 1–20) and stitch fabric 1 to fabric 20 on the bottom of the segment from step 2.
4. On another slice, remove the stitching between fabrics 18 and 19 to make a two-fabric segment. Stitch fabric 19 to fabric 20 on the bottom of the partial row from step 3.

5. On the remaining segment from step 4, remove the stitching between fabrics 16 and 17 *and* between fabrics 6 and 7. Use the segment with fabrics 7–16 and stitch fabric 16 to fabric 20 at the bottom of the partial row from step 4. Fabric 7 will now be at the bottom of the row.

6. Using the segment with fabrics 1–6 from step 5, stitch fabric 1 to fabric 7 at the bottom of the row. Fabric 6 will now be at the bottom of the row.

7. On the leftover segment from step 2, remove the stitching between fabrics 5 and 6. Stitch fabric 1 to fabric 6 at the bottom of the row. You now have a complete row. In the same manner, make a second identical row 2.

8. Compare the two rows to each other and to the chart for accuracy. Press all seam allowances toward the even-numbered fabrics.

9. Lay the rows on your ironing board side by side with row 1 in the middle. They should all be the same length and in the number sequence indicated on the chart.

Joining the rows

Sew a row 2 to either side of row 1 before assembling row 3.

1. With right sides together and raw edges aligned, place row 2 on top of row 1. Using a scant ¼"-wide seam allowance and starting at the top of the row, join the rows along their long edges, carefully matching the seam intersections with your finger. You may want to use a stylus or an awl to hold the matched seam intersections in place, gently easing the fabric as needed to align the seams.

2. Press the seam allowances toward the newly added row—away from the center of the quilt—before sewing the second row 2.

3. Place the second row 2 on top of row 1, right sides together and raw edges aligned. Starting at the bottom of the row, join the rows along their long edges, carefully matching the seam intersections.

LEFTOVER SEGMENTS

Keep track of your leftover segments by pinning them to a corner of your design wall or to a small foam board, grouping segments from slices of equal width together. Then they are easily viewed for later use in this quilt or in "Sunset Strippy Quilt" on page 65, designed specifically to utilize the leftover bits.

Working from the Chart

1. Continue working in this manner, for each pair of rows cut six slices in the width indicated on the chart. Referring to your fabric map and using the bold lines on the chart as a guide, remove the stitching between segments, as needed, and join the segments in the order indicated on the chart for the row you're making. You'll be making two identical rows each time.

2. After completing each new pair of rows, check that they match the chart and that they're the same length as the center section.

3. Join each new pair of rows to opposite sides of the center section, alternating the stitching direction and pressing the seam allowances toward the newly added rows before working on the next pair of rows.

Creating Additional Sections

Once you've completed and added row 10 to each side, you might want to begin two new sections, each with rows 11–27. I find that dividing the project into three sections makes it easier to handle.

1. Continue working in the same manner as described before until you've worked all the way across the chart, adding identical rows to each side of the center. Make sure you have a right side and a mirror-image left side that can be joined to the center section to complete the symmetrical design.

2. To complete rows 18–20, use leftover segments for the bottom pieces beginning with fabric 19 in row 18.

3. Join the three sections in the correct numerical order to complete your quilt top. Check the back of the quilt top, correct any seam allowances that aren't lying flat, and press them in the proper direction.

4. Finish by basting around the quilt top about ⅛" from the outer edges to stabilize the seams for quilting.

Finishing

For more details on any of the following steps, go to ShopMartingale.com/HowtoQuilt for free downloadable information.

1. Layer the quilt top with batting and backing. Baste and quilt as desired. (Or take the neatly folded quilt top and backing to your professional long-arm machine quilter.)

2. Using the 2¼"-wide binding strips, make and attach the binding.

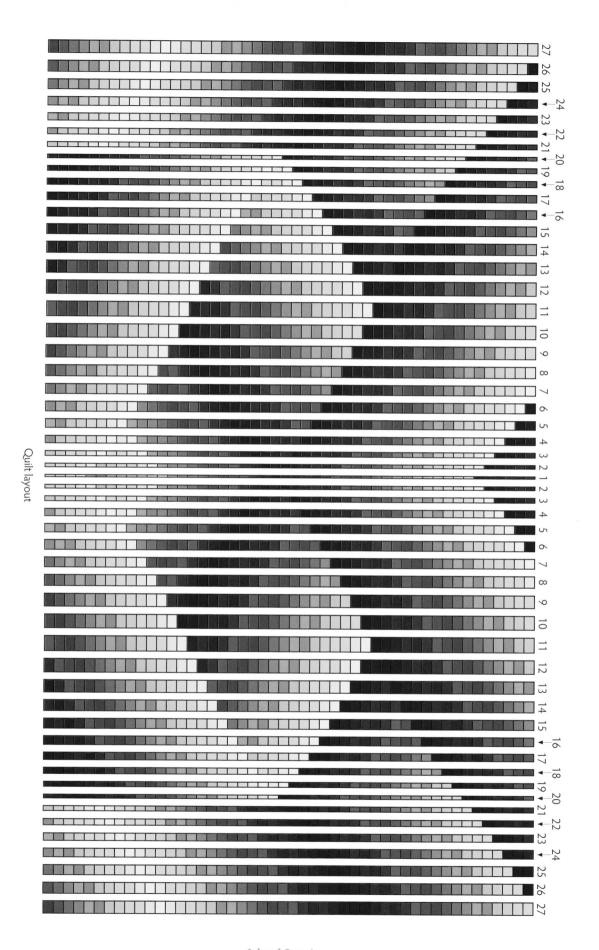

Quilt layout

27
26 25
24
23
22
21 20
19
18
17
16
15
14
13
12
11
10
9
8
7
6
5
4
3
2
1
1
2
3
4
5
6
7
8
9
10
11
12
13
14 15
16
17
18
19 20
21
22
23
24
25
26
27

Island Sunrise

ISLAND SUNRISE DESIGN CHART

Begin working with row 1 (far right), which is the center of the quilt. Make two of each subsequent row and place them on either side of the quilt center so that the design forms a mirror image.

	27	26	25	24	23	22	21	20	19	18	17	16	15	14	13	12	11	10	9	8	7	6	5	4	3	2	1
Row number	27	26	25	24	23	22	21	20	19	18	17	16	15	14	13	12	11	10	9	8	7	6	5	4	3	2	1
Cut width of row	3"	2¾"	2½"	2¼"	2"	1¾"	1½"	1"	1½"	1¾"	2"	2¼"	2½"	2¾"	3"	3¼"	3½"	3¼"	3"	2¾"	2½"	2½"	2¼"	2"	1½"	1¼"	1"
Fabric number	3	20	19	18	17	16	15	14	13	12	11	10	9	8	7	6	5	4	3	2	1	20	19	18	17	16	15
	4	3	20	19	18	17	16	15	14	13	12	11	10	9	8	7	6	5	4	3	2	1	20	19	18	17	16
	5	4	3	20	19	18	17	16	15	14	13	12	11	10	9	8	7	6	5	4	3	2	1	20	19	18	17
	6	5	4	3	20	19	18	17	16	15	14	13	12	11	10	9	8	7	6	5	4	3	2	1	20	19	18
	7	6	5	4	3	20	19	18	17	16	15	14	13	12	11	10	9	8	7	6	5	4	3	2	1	20	19
	8	7	6	5	4	3	20	19	18	17	16	15	14	13	12	11	10	9	8	7	6	5	4	3	2	1	20
	9	8	7	6	5	4	3	20	19	18	17	16	15	14	13	12	11	10	9	8	7	6	5	4	3	2	1
	10	9	8	7	6	5	4	3	20	19	18	17	16	15	14	13	12	11	10	9	8	7	6	5	4	3	2
	11	10	9	8	7	6	5	4	5	20	19	18	17	16	15	14	13	12	11	10	9	8	7	6	5	4	3
	12	11	10	9	8	7	6	5	6	7	20	19	18	17	16	15	14	13	12	11	10	9	8	7	6	5	4
	13	12	11	10	9	8	7	6	7	8	9	20	19	18	17	16	15	14	13	12	11	10	9	8	7	6	5
	14	13	12	11	10	9	8	7	8	9	10	11	20	19	18	17	16	15	14	13	12	11	10	9	8	7	6
	15	14	13	12	11	10	9	8	9	10	11	12	13	20	19	18	17	16	15	14	13	12	11	10	9	8	7
	16	15	14	13	12	11	10	9	10	11	12	13	14	15	20	19	18	17	16	15	14	13	12	11	10	9	8
	17	16	15	14	13	12	11	10	11	12	13	14	15	16	17	20	19	18	17	16	15	14	13	12	11	10	9
	18	17	16	15	14	13	12	11	12	13	14	15	16	17	18	19	20	19	18	17	16	15	14	13	12	11	10
	19	18	17	16	15	14	13	12	13	14	15	16	17	18	19	20	1	20	19	18	17	16	15	14	13	12	11
	20	19	18	17	16	15	14	13	14	15	16	17	18	19	20	1	2	3	20	19	18	17	16	15	14	13	12
	19	20	19	18	17	16	15	14	15	16	17	18	19	20	1	2	3	4	5	20	19	18	17	16	15	14	13
	18	19	20	19	18	17	16	15	16	17	18	19	20	1	2	3	4	5	6	7	20	19	18	17	16	15	14
	17	18	19	20	19	18	17	16	17	18	19	20	1	2	3	4	5	6	7	8	9	20	19	18	17	16	15
	16	17	18	19	20	19	18	17	18	19	20	1	2	3	4	5	6	7	8	9	10	11	20	19	18	17	16
	15	16	17	18	19	20	19	18	19	20	1	2	3	4	5	6	7	8	9	10	11	12	13	20	19	18	17
	14	15	16	17	18	19	20	19	20	1	2	3	4	5	6	7	8	9	10	11	12	13	14	15	20	19	18
	13	14	15	16	17	18	19	20	1	2	3	4	5	6	7	8	9	10	11	12	13	14	15	16	17	20	19
	12	13	14	15	16	17	18	1	2	3	4	5	6	7	8	9	10	11	12	13	14	15	16	17	18	19	20
	11	12	13	14	15	16	17	2	1	4	5	6	7	8	9	10	11	12	13	14	15	16	17	18	19	20	16
	10	11	12	13	14	15	16	3	2	1	6	7	8	9	10	11	12	13	14	15	16	17	18	19	20	16	15
	9	10	11	12	13	14	15	5	4	3	2	1	8	9	10	11	12	13	14	15	16	17	18	19	20	16	14
	8	9	10	11	12	13	14	5	4	3	2	1	10	11	12	13	14	15	16	17	18	19	20	16	15	14	13
	7	8	9	10	11	12	13	6	5	4	3	2	1	12	13	14	15	16	17	18	19	20	16	15	14	13	12
	6	7	8	9	10	11	12	7	6	5	4	3	2	1	14	15	16	17	18	19	20	16	15	14	13	12	11
	5	6	7	8	9	10	11	8	7	6	5	4	3	2	1	16	17	18	19	20	16	15	14	13	12	11	10
	4	5	6	7	8	9	10	9	10	7	6	5	4	3	2	1	18	19	20	16	15	14	13	12	11	10	9
	3	4	5	6	7	8	9	10	9	8	7	6	5	4	3	2	1	20	16	15	14	13	12	11	10	9	8
	2	3	4	5	6	7	8	11	10	9	8	7	6	5	4	3	2	1	15	14	13	12	11	10	9	8	7
	1	2	3	4	5	6	7	12	11	10	9	8	7	6	5	4	3	2	1	13	12	11	10	9	8	7	1
	2	1	2	3	4	5	6	13	12	11	10	9	8	7	6	5	4	3	2	1	11	10	9	8	7	1	2
	3	2	1	2	3	4	5	14	13	12	11	10	9	8	7	6	5	4	3	2	1	9	8	7	1	2	3
	4	3	2	1	2	3	4	15	14	13	12	11	10	9	8	7	6	5	4	3	2	1	7	1	2	3	4
	5	4	3	2	1	2	3	16	15	14	13	12	11	10	9	8	7	6	5	4	3	2	1	2	3	4	5
	6	5	4	3	2	1	2	17	16	15	14	13	12	11	10	9	8	7	6	5	4	3	2	1	4	5	6
	7	6	5	4	3	2	1	18	17	16	15	14	13	12	11	10	9	8	7	6	5	4	3	2	1	6	7
	8	7	6	5	4	3	2	19	18	17	16	15	14	13	12	11	10	9	8	7	6	5	4	3	2	1	8
	9	8	7	6	5	4	3	20	19	18	17	16	15	14	13	12	11	10	9	8	7	6	5	4	3	2	1
	10	9	8	7	6	5	4	19	20	19	18	17	16	15	14	13	12	11	10	9	8	7	6	5	4	3	2
	11	10	9	8	7	6	5	18	19	20	19	18	17	16	15	14	13	12	11	10	9	8	7	6	5	4	3
	12	11	10	9	8	7	6	17	18	19	20	19	18	17	16	15	14	13	12	11	10	9	8	7	6	5	4

Island Sunrise

Sunset Strippy Quilt

"Sunset Strippy Quilt" cried out to be made when I saw how many segments were left over after making "Island Sunrise" on page 59. Thanks to my friends, the Wayward Quilters, for the quilt name. Thanks also to Gail Stenberg for the professional quilting job on her long-arm machine.

Choosing Fabric

Select seven leftover fabrics (at least 7" x 35") from "Island Sunrise" or choose seven new fabrics that coordinate with your leftover segments.

Materials

Yardage is based on 42"-wide fabric.

1¾ yards of coordinating dark fabric for borders and binding

¼ yard *each* of 7 fabrics for blocks

3½ yards of fabric for backing

60" x 69" piece of batting

Cutting

From *each* of the 7 fabrics for blocks, cut:

1 strip, 6½" x 42"; crosscut into 5 squares, 6½" x 6½"

From the dark fabric for borders and binding, cut:

6 strips, 2½" x 42"

7 strips, 3½" x 42"

7 strips, 2¼" x 42"

Making the Quilt Center

1. On a design wall, position the squares in seven rows of five squares each, leaving 2½" between the squares on all sides. Refer to the photo on page 66 and the quilt layout diagram as needed.

2. Using leftover segments from "Island Sunrise," trim any 3½"- to 2¾"-wide segments to 2½" wide. Remove the stitching on the leftover segments as needed to make 42 three-fabric segments. (You can also join shorter segments and then remove the stitching to make three-fabric segments.) Set aside any leftover single pieces of fabric for the next step. Arrange the segments vertically between the squares and at the beginning and end of each row.

3. Cut the leftover strip sets (fabrics 1–20) into eight 2½"-wide segments. Add one 2½" piece of fabric to one end to make a 21-fabric sashing strip. (You can also join shorter segments to make 21-fabric strips.) Position the sashing strips horizontally between the rows of squares, starting and ending with a sashing strip. Rearrange the squares, segments, and strips until you're pleased with the layout.

Pieced by author and machine quilted by Gail Stenberg of Nanaimo, British Columbia, Canada

FINISHED SIZE: 54½" x 63½"

Sunset Strippy Quilt

4. Sew the vertical segments and the squares together to make seven rows. Press the seam allowances toward the squares.

5. Join the rows from step 4 and the sashing strips to complete the quilt center. Press the seam allowances away from the sashing strips.

Borders and Finishing

For more details on any of the following steps, go to ShopMartingale.com/HowtoQuilt for free download-able information.

1. Trim the remaining leftover segments to 1½"-wide for the middle border. Join the 1½"-wide segments to make a 275"-long strip.

2. Join like border strips to make a dark 2½"-wide single strip and a dark 3½"-wide single strip. Sew the dark border strips to opposite sides of

the pieced border strip from step 1 to make a border unit. Press the seam allowances toward the dark borders.

Border unit

3. Measure, cut, and sew the border unit to the quilt top. Miter the corners.

4. Layer the quilt top with batting and backing. Baste and quilt as desired. (Or take the neatly folded quilt top and backing to your professional long-arm machine quilter.)

5. Using the 2¼"-wide binding strips, make and attach the binding.

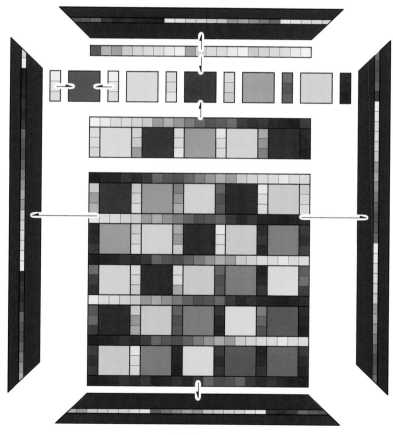

Quilt layout

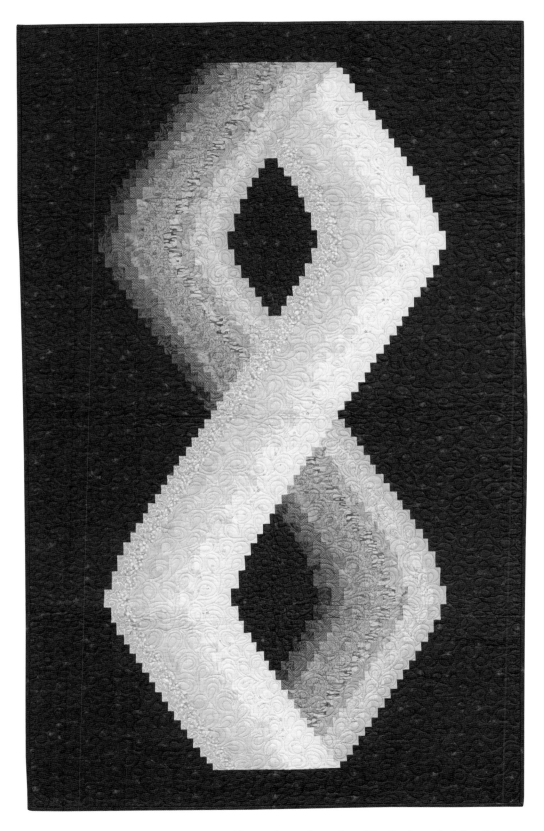

Pieced by author and machine quilted by Nadia Wilson, Port Hardy, British Columbia, Canada

FINISHED SIZE: 63¼" x 38½"

Möbius

Not only was this the hardest quilt to make but also the hardest to chart by number so you could make it too. This image has danced in my head for years, so when other quilters requested a möbius design, it just had to happen. Choosing colors that looked best on a brown background also proved to be challenging, but these soft peaches, tans, and beiges seem to do the trick.

Choosing Fabric

You'll need 20 fabrics in one color family for the ribbon: 10 light fabrics and 10 dark fabrics. The fabrics in each group should range from light to dark. You'll also need a dark background fabric that shows off the ribbon colors to their best advantage.

Materials

Yardage is based on 42"-wide fabric.

¼ yard *each* of 10 light fabrics for the bargello ribbon
⅛ yard *each* of 10 dark fabrics for the bargello ribbon
2⅝ yards of dark fabric for ribbon background, borders, and binding
2⅞ yards of fabric for backing
44" x 69" piece of batting

Fabric Map

Referring to page 8, use a scrap of each bargello fabric to create a fabric map. You'll need to refer to your map throughout the project in order to position all of the strips correctly to make the design shown.

Cutting

From *each* of the 10 light bargello fabrics, cut:
3 strips, 1½" x 42"

From *each* of the 10 dark bargello fabrics, cut:
2 strips, 1½" x 42"

From the dark fabric for ribbon background, borders, and binding, cut:
4 strips, 1" x 42"
31 strips, 1¼" x 42"
10 strips, 1½" x 42"
2 strips, 1¾" x 42"
2 strips, 2" x 42"
2 strips, 3½" x 42"
6 strips, 2¼" x 42"

CUTTING BACKGROUND PIECES

For this quilt, I recommend that you cut the required background pieces at the top and bottom of the row as you build each row. The letter B on the "Möbius Design Chart" (pages 72–75) refers to a section of background fabric. Referring to the chart and using a background strip in the required width, cut two strips in the length indicated for the top and bottom of each row.

Making the Strip Sets

1. Referring to "Building Strip Sets" on page 9 and using the 10 light bargello fabric strips, sew the strips together in numerical order according to your fabric map to make three identical strip sets. Press the seam allowances toward fabric 10.

2. In the same manner, use the 10 dark bargello fabric strips to make two identical strips sets. Press the seam allowances toward fabric 11.

Fabric 1	Fabric 11
Fabric 2	Fabric 12
Fabric 3	Fabric 13
Fabric 4	Fabric 14
Fabric 5	Fabric 15
Fabric 6	Fabric 16
Fabric 7	Fabric 17
Fabric 8	Fabric 18
Fabric 9	Fabric 19
Fabric 10	Fabric 20

Make 3.   Make 2.

3. Sew eight of the 1½" x 42" background strips together into one strip set. Press the seam allowances in one direction.

BACKGROUND-FABRIC STRIP SET

Why do you need to make a strip set with background strips instead of using a single strip of fabric cut to the width and length required? The smallest differences in sewing and pressing can affect the length of the piece you're making. Using pieced segments to connect the ribbon slices will make building the rows easier and ensure accuracy. If you use a single strip cut to length on the top and bottom of each row, you may need to trim the outer edges before adding the binding.

Row 1

1. From a 1"-wide background strip, cut two 14½"-long strips.

2. From a strip set with fabrics 11–20, cut one 1"-wide slice. Refer to "Cutting Slices" on page 11 as needed for guidance.

3. Sew one background strip from step 1 to fabric 11 and the other background strip to fabric 20 to complete row 1. Press the seam allowances toward the top of the row.

4. Using your fabric map as a guide, compare your finished row to row 1 on the chart. The numbers assigned to your fabrics should be in the same order as the chart numbers for row 1.

Row 2

1. From a 1"-wide background strip, cut two 14"-long strips.

2. From a strip set with fabrics 11–20, cut one 1"-wide slice.

3. From a strip set with fabrics 1–10, cut one 1"-wide slice. Remove the stitching between fabrics 1 and 2 to create a single piece of fabric. Set aside the remaining segment for possible use later.

4. Sew the single fabric piece (fabric 1) to fabric 11 on the segment from step 2. Fabric 1 will be the top of the row.

5. Sew one background strip from step 1 to fabric 1 and the other background strip to fabric 20 to complete row 2. Press the seam allowances toward the top of the row.

6. Using your fabric map as a guide, compare your finished row to row 2 on the chart. The numbers assigned to your fabrics should be in the same order as the chart numbers for row 2. Compare the two rows to each other; they should be the same length.

Joining Rows

With right sides together and raw edges aligned, place row 2 on top of row 1. Align the top and bottom edges and stagger the seam lines ½", matching the midpoint on each strip in row 2 with the seam line on row 1, as described in "Stepping Down" on page 54. Using a scant ¼"-wide seam allowance, join the rows along their long edges, gently easing the fabric as needed. Press the seam allowances toward the newly added row, in this case row 2.

Working from the Chart

1. Continue working in the same manner, cutting slices and building one row at a time, working across the chart. Referring to your fabric map and using the chart as a guide, remove the stitching between segments, as needed, and join the segments in the order indicated for the row you're making. You may be able to use some of the leftover segments to complete the rows.

2. For rows 12–24 and rows 46–58, you need to cut slices in the width indicated on the chart from the background strip set. The number of slices you'll need will depend on the row you're building and how many leftover background segments you can utilize. Remove the stitching between fabrics, as needed, to make the segments indicated on the chart (for example, B6 means you'll need a six-fabric background segment). Referring to your fabric map, join the background segments and ribbon segments in the order indicated for the row you're making.

3. Once you've completed and joined 17 rows, you might want to begin a new section with rows 18–34; then build two additional sections for rows 35–51 and rows 52–69. Dividing the project into four sections makes it easier to handle.

4. After completing each new row, check that it matches the chart, and that the seam allowances are all pressed in the same direction.

5. Join each new row to the section you're constructing and press the seam allowances toward the newly added row.

ABOUT THE DESIGN CHART

The blank areas on the design chart on pages 72–75 do not represent fabric sections. Because the rows in this quilt are stepped up or down half of the strip width, the blank areas are needed to establish the design. For rows 6–10, rows 25–29, rows 41–45, and rows 59–63, simply join the last number to the next number in each row.

Assembly

1. Join the four sections in the correct numerical order to complete the center of your quilt top.

2. Measure the length of the quilt top through the center. Cut two dark 3½"-wide strips to this length. Pin and sew the strips to the sides of the quilt top. Press the seam allowances toward the border strips.

3. Finish by basting along the top and bottom of the quilt top about ⅛" from the outer edges to stabilize the seams for quilting.

Finishing

For more details on any of the following steps, go to ShopMartingale.com/HowtoQuilt for free downloadable information.

1. Layer the quilt top with batting and backing. Baste and quilt as desired. (Or take the neatly folded quilt top and backing to your professional long-arm machine quilter.)

2. Using the 2¼"-wide binding strips, make and attach the binding.

MÖBIUS DESIGN CHART, PART 1

The letter B on the chart refers to a section of background fabric. Use a single strip in the length indicated at the top and bottom of each row, and use the number of pieces indicated from the background strip set to connect the ribbon slices.

Row number	1	2	3	4	5	6	7	8	9	10	11	12	13	14	15	16	17	18	19	20
Cut width of row	1"	1"	1¼"	1¼"	1¼"	1¼"	1¼"	1¼"	1¼"	1¼"	1¼"	1¼"	1¼"	1¼"	1½"	1¾"	2"	2"	1¾"	1½"
Fabric number	B14½"	B14"	B13½"	B13"	B12½"	B12"	B11½"	B11"	B10½"	B10"	B9½"	B9"	B8½"	B8"	B7½"	B7"	B6½"	B6"	B6½"	B7"
																		1		
																	1	2	1	
																1	2	3	2	1
															1	2	3	4	3	2
														1	2	3	4	5	4	3
													1	2	3	4	5	6	5	4
												1	2	3	4	5	6	7	6	5
											1	2	3	4	5	6	7	8	7	6
										1	2	3	4	5	6	7	8	9	8	7
									1	2	3	4	5	6	7	8	9	10	9	8
								1	2	3	4	5	6	7	8	9	10	B7	10	9
							1	2	3	4	5	6	7	8	9	10	B6		B6	10
						1	2	3	4	5	6	7	8	9	10	B5				B5
					1	2	3	4	5	6	7	8	9	10	B4					
				1	2	3	4	5	6	7	8	9	10	B3						
			1	2	3	4	5	6	7	8	9	10	B2							
		1	2	3	4	5	6	7	8	9	10	B1								
	11	11	11	11	11	11														
	12	12	12	12	12	12	11													
	13	13	13	13	13	13	12	11												
	14	14	14	14	14	14	13	12	11											
	15	15	15	15	15	15	14	13	12	11										
	16	16	16	16	16	16	15	14	13	12	11									
	17	17	17	17	17	17	16	15	14	13	12	11								
	18	18	18	18	18	18	17	16	15	14	13	12	11							
	19	19	19	19	19	19	18	17	16	15	14	13	12	11						
	20	20	20	20	20	20	19	18	17	16	15	14	13	12	11					
	B14½"	B14"	B13½"	B13"	B12½"	B12"	20	19	18	17	16	15	14	13	12	11				11
							B11½"	20	19	18	17	16	15	14	13	12	11		11	12
								B11"	20	19	18	17	16	15	14	13	12	11	12	13
									B10½"	20	19	18	17	16	15	14	13	12	13	14
										B10"	20	19	18	17	16	15	14	13	14	15
											B9½"	20	19	18	17	16	15	14	15	16
												B9"	20	19	18	17	16	15	16	17
													B8½"	20	19	18	17	16	17	18
														B8"	20	19	18	17	18	19
															B7½"	20	19	18	19	20
																B7"	20	19	20	B7"
																	B6½"	20	B6½"	
																		B6"		

MÖBIUS DESIGN CHART, PART 2

The letter B on the chart refers to a section of background fabric. Use a single strip in the length indicated at the top and bottom of each row, and use the number of pieces indicated from the background strip set to connect the ribbon slices.

Row number	21	22	23	24	25	26	27	28	29	30	31	32	33	34	35	36	37	38	39	40
Cut width of row	1¼"	1¼"	1¼"	1¼"	1¼"	1¼"	1¼"	1¼"	1¼"	1¼"	1¼"	1¼"	1¼"	1¼"	1¼"	1¼"	1¼"	1¼"	1¼"	1¼"
Fabric number	B7½"	B8"	B8½"	B9"	B9½"	B10"	B10½"	B11"	B11½"	B12"	B12½"	B13"	B13½"	B14"	B14½"	B14"	B13½"	B13"	B12½"	B12"
	1																			
	2	1																		
	3	2	1																	
	4	3	2	1																
	5	4	3	2	1															
	6	5	4	3	2	1														
	7	6	5	4	3	2	1													
	8	7	6	5	4	3	2	1												
	9	8	7	6	5	4	3	2	1											
	10	9	8	7	6	5	4	3	2	1										11
	B4	10	9	8	7	6	5	4	3	2	1								11	12
		B3	10	9	8	7	6	5	4	3	2	1						11	12	13
			B2	10	9	8	7	6	5	4	3	2	1				11	12	13	14
				B1	10	9	8	7	6	5	4	3	2	1		11	12	13	14	15
						10	9	8	7	6	5	4	3	2	1	1	1	1	1	1
							10	9	8	7	6	5	4	3	2	2	2	2	2	2
								10	9	8	7	6	5	4	3	3	3	3	3	3
									10	9	8	7	6	5	4	4	4	4	4	4
										10	9	8	7	6	5	5	5	5	5	5
					11	12	13	14	15	16	10	9	8	7	6	6	6	6	6	6
				11	12	13	14	15	16	17	17	10	9	8	7	7	7	7	7	7
			11	12	13	14	15	16	17	18	18	18	10	9	8	8	8	8	8	8
		11	12	13	14	15	16	17	18	19	19	19	19	10	9	9	9	9	9	9
	11	12	13	14	15	16	17	18	19	20	20	20	20	20	10	10	10	10	10	10
	12	13	14	15	16	17	18	19	20	B12"	B12½"	B13"	B13½"	B14"	B14½"	B14"	B13½"	B13"	B12½"	B12"
	13	14	15	16	17	18	19	20	B11½"											
	14	15	16	17	18	19	20	B11"												
	15	16	17	18	19	20	B10½"													
	16	17	18	19	20	B10"														
	17	18	19	20	B9½"															
	18	19	20	B9"																
	19	20	B8½"																	
	20	B8"																		
	B7½"																			

MÖBIUS DESIGN CHART, PART 3

The letter B on the chart refers to a section of background fabric. Use a single strip in the length indicated at the top and bottom of each row, and use the number of pieces indicated from the background strip set to connect the ribbon slices.

Row number	41	42	43	44	45	46	47	48	49	50	51	52	53	54	55	56	57	58	59	60
Cut width of row	1¼"	1¼"	1¼"	1¼"	1¼"	1¼"	1¼"	1¼"	1½"	1¾"	2"	2"	1¾"	1½	1¼"	1¼"	1¼"	1¼"	1¼"	1¼"
Fabric number	B11½"	B11"	B10½"	B10"	B9½"	B9"	B8½"	B8"	B7½"	B7"	B6½"	B6"	B6½"	B7"	B7½"	B8"	B8½"	B9"	B9½"	B10"
												11								
											11	12	11							
										11	12	13	12	11						
									11	12	13	14	13	12	11					
								11	12	13	14	15	14	13	12	11				
							11	12	13	14	15	16	15	14	13	12	11			
						11	12	13	14	15	16	17	16	15	14	13	12	11		
					11	12	13	14	15	16	17	18	17	16	15	14	13	12	11	
				11	12	13	14	15	16	17	18	19	18	17	16	15	14	13	12	11
			11	12	13	14	15	16	17	18	19	20	19	18	17	16	15	14	13	12
		11	12	13	14	15	16	17	18	19	20	B7	20	19	18	17	16	15	14	13
	11	12	13	14	15	16	17	18	19	20	B6		B6	20	19	18	17	16	15	14
	12	13	14	15	16	17	18	19	20	B5				B5	20	19	18	17	16	15
	13	14	15	16	17	18	19	20	B4						B4	20	19	18	17	16
	14	15	16	17	18	19	20	B3								B3	20	19	18	17
	15	16	17	18	19	20	B2										B2	20	19	18
	16	17	18	19	20	B1												B1	20	19
	1																			
	2	1																		
	3	2	1																	
	4	3	2	1																1
	5	4	3	2	1														1	2
	6	5	4	3	2	1												1	2	3
	7	6	5	4	3	2	1										1	2	3	4
	8	7	6	5	4	3	2	1								1	2	3	4	5
	9	8	7	6	5	4	3	2	1						1	2	3	4	5	6
	10	9	8	7	6	5	4	3	2	1				1	2	3	4	5	6	7
	B11½"	10	9	8	7	6	5	4	3	2	1		1	2	3	4	5	6	7	8
		B11"	10	9	8	7	6	5	4	3	2	1	2	3	4	5	6	7	8	9
			B10½"	10	9	8	7	6	5	4	3	2	3	4	5	6	7	8	9	10
				B10"	10	9	8	7	6	5	4	3	4	5	6	7	8	9	10	B10"
					B9½"	10	9	8	7	6	5	4	5	6	7	8	9	10	B9½"	
						B9"	10	9	8	7	6	5	6	7	8	9	10	B9"		
							B8½"	10	9	8	7	6	7	8	9	10	B8½"			
								B8"	10	9	8	7	8	9	10	B8"				
									B7½"	10	9	8	9	10	B7½"					
										B7"	10	9	10	B7"						
											B6½"	10	B6½"							
												B6"								

MÖBIUS DESIGN CHART, PART 4

The letter B on the chart refers to a section of background fabric. Use a single strip in the length indicated at the top and bottom of each row.

Row number	61	62	63	64	65	66	67	68	69
Cut width of row	1¼"	1¼"	1¼"	1¼"	1¼"	1¼"	1¼"	1"	1"
Fabric number	B10½"	B11"	B11½"	B12"	B12½"	B13"	B13½"	B14"	B14½"
	12								
	13	12							
	14	13	12						
	15	14	13	12					
	16	15	14	13	12				
	17	16	15	14	13	12			
	18	17	16	15	14	13	12	11	
				1	1	1	1	1	1
			1	2	2	2	2	2	2
		1	2	3	3	3	3	3	3
	1	2	3	4	4	4	4	4	4
	2	3	4	5	5	5	5	5	5
	3	4	5	6	6	6	6	6	6
	4	5	6	7	7	7	7	7	7
	5	6	7	8	8	8	8	8	8
	6	7	8	9	9	9	9	9	9
	7	8	9	10	10	10	10	10	10
	8	9	10	B12"	B12½"	B13"	B13½"	B14"	B14½"
	9	10	B11½"						
	10	B11"							
	B10½"								

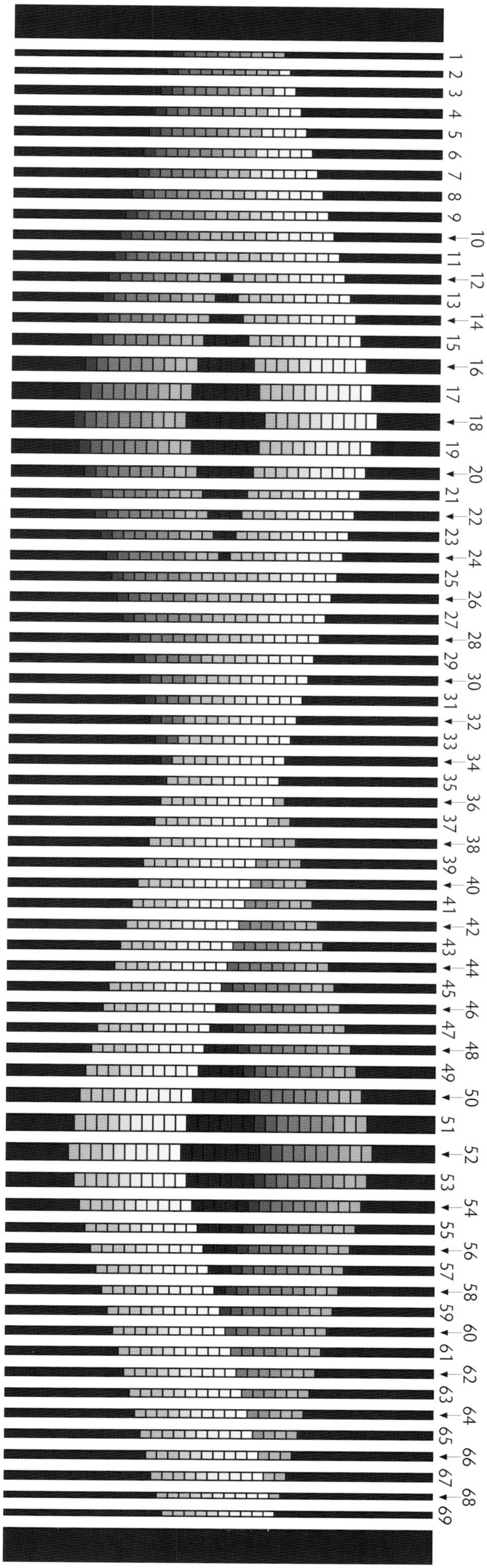

Möbius

Quilt layout

Bargello for Baby by Kelli Banks, Victoria, British Columbia, Canada; machine quilted by Jan Symonds

Kelli and I were on a quilting retreat soon after I designed "Bargello for Baby" (page 13). Her yellow-and-teal version is quite cheerful!

Bargello Bed Runner by Carol Thompson, Kilarney, Manitoba, Canada; machine quilted by Gail Stenberg, Nanaimo, British Columbia, Canada

Carol is a member of the Wayward Quilters and learned strip piecing from me. Since her daughters gave me the idea for a bed runner, I convinced her to make her own version of the project. Unfortunately for them, they won't be getting the bed runner—Carol is keeping it!

Hawaiian Tide by Laurel Heal, Victoria, British Columbia, Canada; machine quilted by Nancy McIntyre

After seeing "Surf Song" from my first book hanging in a quilt-shop window, Laurel wanted to try her hand at bargello. With a bit of direction on choosing fabrics, Laurel completed her very first quilt, and I'm thrilled to have it in this book to prove that bargello really isn't that hard!

Sahara Sunrise by Marilyn Fuller, Victoria, British Columbia, Canada

Based on sunrise colors in an entirely different corner of the world, Marilyn's quilt was inspired by the many colors of sunrises on the Sahara Desert as seen from the Hubbell space station. Inspiration can come from anywhere.

Glacier Bay Sunset by Alice Duncan,
Victoria, British Columbia, Canada;
machine quilted by Nancy McIntyre

*Alice captured the beauty of glaciers, particularly
at sunset, in this stunning quilt.*

Argyle by Jennifer Mummery, East Sooke,
British Columbia, Canada

*Jennifer quilted my green "Argyle" quilt, and
then turned around and made her own version
in shades of brown and cream for herself. This
is Jennifer's first bargello quilt, and it won the
Canadian Quilter's Association Award, Best
in Show, and first place in its category at the
Westshore Quilter's Guild show, "It Started
with a Stitch."*

Rhapsody in Red by Fran Henney, Parksville, British Columbia, Canada

"Island Sunset" was Fran's favorite quilt in my first book. When I decided to create it in queen size for my second book, she was thrilled. Then, Fran discovered the "French General" fabric collection by Moda, and she was in love. It took her several months to find 20 different fabrics in the fabric collection, but after going to every Vancouver Island quilt shop, plus many in Washington and Oregon, she had gathered 30 fabrics. She picked 20 of her favorite fabrics for this quilt.

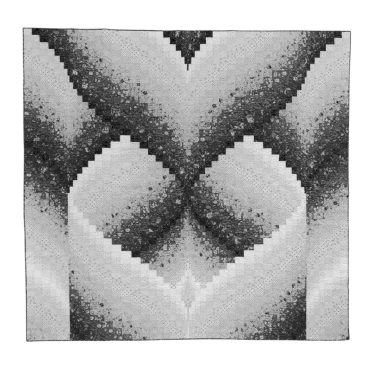

Berries on Ice by Donna Mighton, Nanaimo, British Columbia, Canada; machine quilted by Fran Henney, Parksville, British Columbia, Canada

Donna started her quilt in the spring when the raspberries, blueberries, and elderberries first blossom, and the quilt continued to grow, as did the berries, through summer and fall. From blossoms to ripe berries waiting for harvest before the ice forms on the lakes and rivers, this quilt follows the berries' journey—as well as the journey of life.

Acknowledgments

A special thank-you to the ladies in my Wednesday quilting group, the Wayward Quilters. Your advice and support kept me moving forward when I felt stuck and discouraged. You helped name the quilts and photograph them for my editors, all while keeping me smiling. And you're such good cooks. It is hard to diet in your company.

Thank you to my technical editor, Nancy Mahoney, for making sure my math was accurate and keeping the instructions clear and concise. And to Martingale for making another book of mine so very beautiful and for being my publisher. You are the best.

I must also acknowledge all the quilters who so eagerly agreed to test my instructions and make a sample for the gallery of this book. Your quilts are beautiful and sometimes I even like your color choices better than my own. Also thank you to my long-arm quilters, Fran Henney, Jennifer Mummery, Gail Stenberg, and Nadia Wilson, who humored me when every job of mine was rush. Your talents always make my quilts look better. I am grateful to have all of you in my life.

About the Author

Eileen Wright relocated to Parksville, British Columbia, on Vancouver Island a couple of years ago where she loves the small-town feel and the close proximity to the ocean. She claims her new career will be quilting up her stash to make comfort quilts for neglected seniors in care homes and little ones who need a hug. Eileen enjoys the ocean and organizing and attending quilting retreats when she isn't quilting at home or with her friends. She still does a bit of teaching to share her techniques, but would like to think that she has retired. Eileen was recently reunited with her many siblings, which has added even more joy to her life.